THE WATTA-DWELLERS
A Sociological Study of Selected Urban Low-Income Communities in Sri Lanka

Kalinga Tudor Silva
Karunatissa Athukorala

Department of Sociology
University of Peradeniya
Peradeniya
Sri Lanka

UNIVERSITY
PRESS OF
AMERICA

Lanham • New York • London

Copyright © 1991 by

University Press of America®, Inc.

4720 Boston Way
Lanham, Maryland 20706

3 Henrietta Street
London WC2E 8LU England

Library of Congress Cataloging-in-Publication Data

Silva, Kalinga Tudor, 1949-
The watta-dwellers : a sociological study of selected
urban low—income communities in Sri Lanka
/ Kalinga Tudor Silva, Karunatissa Athukorala.
p.   cm.
Includes bibliographical references (p.) and index.
1. Urban poor—Sri Lanka—Case studies.
2. Slums—Sri Lanka—Case studies.
I. Athukorala, Karunatissa.   II. Title.
HV4132.8.A5S57   1990
307.3'36416'095493—dc20   90-24260 CIP

ISBN 0–8191–8106–4 (cloth : alk. paper)

CONTENTS

PREFACE

This work provides a first-hand account of the social life in four selected urban low-income communities in Sri Lanka, locally known as the wattas. The communities studied consisted of one slum and one shanty community in Colombo, one slum in Kandy and, finally, a community of mixed character in Negombo. In each watta community intensive ethnographic research was conducted by a trained sociologist under the guidance and supervision of a Principal Investigator for a period of six to nine months covering late 1983 and early 1984. Thus the "ethnographic present" described in this work refers to the period following the wave of ethnic violence that spread across Sri Lanka in July 1983, unleashed, among others, by sections of the urban poor.

The study was supported by a grant from UNICEF. The views expressed and the interpretations made, however, are entirely the responsibility of the research team. The authors gratefully acknowledge the help and encouragement received from Mr. Leo Fonseka and Mr.Rex Casinader who were in charge of the urban programs in UNICEF, Colombo during the early stages of this study. Mr. Franco Sigera, the program officer (urban) in UNICEF, Colombo, proved to be a valuable source of help and advice during the final stages of the study. The authors also express their gratitude to Mr. Eswaran Selvarajah of the National Housing Development Authority and Miss Indranie Hewage of the Common Amenities Board for their cooperation during various stages of the project.

The team of field investigators, consisting of Mr. M.G.M. Razaak, Mr. Palitha Galappaththi, Mr. I. Munasinghe and Mr. Gaminie Wickramasinghe, did an excellent job under difficult circumstances. Several persons including Mrs. Susila Silva, Mrs. Kusum Athukorala, Mr.Vijitha Nanayakkara and Miss Vindupani Ariyawansa helped in the preparation of maps, charts and statistical tables presented in this work. The authors benefited greatly from comments by Professors Jean J. Schensul, Morton Tenzer and K.N.O. Dharmadasa, Dr. George Scott and Mr. Ajith Silva on parts of an earlier draft of the manuscript. We also relied heavily on the excellent computer skills of Mr. Amarasiri de Silva and Mr. Ajith Silva during the preparation of the camera-ready manuscript. Finally, a word of thanks to Miss Renuka Kuruppu for her patience and keenness in preparing the earlier drafts of the typescript.

MAPS

FIGURE

TABLES

ix

x

Chapter 5

Chapter 6

Chapter 7

ABBREVIATIONS

CAB	Common Amenities Board
CDC	Community Development Council
CMC	Colombo Municipal Council
CMPP	Colombo Master Plan Project
FTZ	Free Trade Zone
GCE (OL)	General Certificate of Education, Ordinary Level
GCE (AL)	General Certificate of Education, Advanced Level
JM	Jude Mawatha Community, Colombo
KM	Kamachchode Community, Negombo
KMC	Kandy Municipal Council
MP	Member of Parliament
NGO	Non-Government Organization
NHDA	National Housing Development Authority
PHC	Primary Health Care
PI	Principal Investigator
PWD	Public Works Department
SL	Soyza Lane Community, Kandy
SM	Swarna Mawatha Community, Colombo
UDA	Urban Development Authority
UNICEF	United Nations Children's Fund
UPON	United People's Organization of Negombo
YMCA	Young Men's Christian Association

CHAPTER ONE

INTRODUCTION

It has become necessary to examine closely the urban low-income communities in Sri Lanka and the social processes associated with them for several reasons.

First, according to official estimates, as of 1979, as much as 50 percent of the total population in Colombo, the capital city of Sri Lanka, lived in slums and shanty communities defined according to their housing and neighborhood characteristics (UDA 1979, Ministry of Housing 1983). While the physical conditions in these neighborhoods are quite well known through earlier studies and are generally understood to be in need of improvement, the accompanying social conditions have not been examined satisfactorily, i.e., in a way that is useful to planners, policy makers, program administrators and others concerned about alleviation of poverty in the Third World.

Second, apart from examining the social counterpart of the physical blight associated with these neighborhoods, their social conditions merit attention in their own right. This is because the social processes associated with these neighborhoods tend to overflow into the larger society in their effect if not always in their operation. For instance, in the contemporary Sri Lankan press, the word "underworld" (pathala lokaya) is often used to describe undesirable and at the same time unlawful activities which proliferate in urban low-income neighborhoods. Such "under-

1

world" activities include crime, drug trafficking, gang violence and prostitution, which not only affect the respective urban neighborhoods but also influence the society at large in many different ways. Similarly "political thuggery", an increasingly alarming aspect of contemporary urban politics in Sri Lanka, is believed to have strong connections with certain deprived neighborhoods in each city. There is also a widely-held assumption that the urban poor constitute a major obstacle to planned development and a threat to public health in the urban areas. The maintenance of law and order and the political stability of cities are also affected by a large-scale presence of the urban poor, especially in inner-city areas. All these considerations point to the need to approach entrenched urban poverty as a broad social phenomenon, in addition to examining the physical blight associated with it.

Third, since 1979 the Sri Lankan government has adopted a policy of upgrading the physical conditions in existing urban low-income neighborhoods. A policy declaration in 1979 states,

> The principle should be adopted that wherever possible existing housing stock including slums and shanties should be upgraded rather than destroyed. This principle ensures both an optimal economic use of resources for housing, and minimizes the extent of disruption to residents to whom location is the prime benefit of their present housing (UDA 1979:8).

This policy implies that at least some of the social features of existing urban low-income communities will continue even after physical upgrading. It makes it all the more necessary to understand the fundamental character of the existing slum and shanty communities in urban Sri Lanka.

Fourth, many of the ongoing programs for relieving urban poverty - whether they are directed by government or non-government organizations - utilize a community approach in dealing with urban problems. This is true of various ongoing programs including the Project for Environmental Health and Community Development implemented jointly by the Colombo Municipal Council (CMC) and the Common Amenities Board (CAB) with UNICEF assistance, the various slum and shanty upgrading projects under the National Housing Development Authority (NHDA) and the Urban Development Authority (UDA) and several integrated community development projects conducted in selected urban communities by organizations, such as, U.S. Save the Children, Plan International and the Sarvodaya Movement under its Nagarodaya (awakening of cities) program.

All these projects utilize in one way or the other the existing community structure in slum and shanty neighborhoods as the basis for introducing desired changes in the communities concerned. A thorough knowledge of the social background of the relevant communities is essential for the designing and successful implementation of such programs.

Finally, despite their large number and the increasingly visible role in the emerging socio-political processes in the country, the urban poor have received grossly inadequate attention in recent accounts of Sri Lankan society. Even where it has become necessary to take into account the role of the urban poor, as in recent studies of urban violence in Sri Lanka, certain untested assumptions, such as the following, have been used to describe their conditions.

In the urban places and market towns, an increasing mass of largely **rootless** and

marginally-employed transient population has congregated in slums and bazaars, constituting a ready pool to be mobilized for instant payoffs (Tambiah 1986:52) [emphasis added].

Here it must be admitted that the data are few, but it seems that those mostly involved in the attacks on Tamils were the relatively **rootless urban proletariat** and **semiproletariat** of Colombo (Nissan & Stirrat 1987: 23) [emphasis added].

Sinhalese gangs made up largely of **impoverished and unemployed youth** (<u>rastiyadu karayo</u>, **"aimless troublemakers"**) attacked Tamils in their houses and shops, **settling old scores** and looting...The violence was turned inward among **neighbours** as well as outward to people known only as Tamil. Furthermore, the active rioters, looters and killers were most often from the subordinated classes within the political and economic order. **They turned upon themselves**, human beings subject to the same conditions of life, as well as upon those more politically and economically powerful (Kapferer 1988: 101-102) [emphasis added].

These statements underscore the need to examine the social character of the urban low-income communities in Sri Lanka more closely.

OBJECTIVES OF THE PRESENT STUDY

In view of the considerations noted above, the present study examines the patterns of social life in four selected urban low-income communities in Sri Lanka with a focus on the aspects given below.

4

1. Economy

The employment pattern and the patterns of income
and expenditure in the relevant communities and their
connections with the formal and informal sectors of
the larger economy of the respective towns will be
examined. Besides addressing the question of poverty,
an effort will be made to identify any dynamic and
potentially improvable aspects of their economy. In
this regard, attention will be paid to employment
opportunities in the Middle East, which have of late
emerged as an important avenue of advancement for
those in urban low-income communities in Sri Lanka.

2. Social Organization

The extent to which there is orderly social life
in the relevant communities and the factors underly-
ing any prevailing social order in them will be
studied. The background, distinctive features and the
composition of the relevant communities and any variation among them in regard to these and other aspects
will be analyzed. Both patterns of cooperation and
conflict within these communities will be examined.
Finally, an effort will be made to understand the
specific nature of their involvement in some recent
waves of urban violence in Sri Lanka.

3. Culture

The areas examined under this topic include the
extent to which the inhabitants of these communities
have a distinctive way of life, their specific tastes
in regard to music, films, sports etc. and the
specific nature of their religious beliefs and
practices. Efforts will be made to identify any
dynamic and adaptable aspects of their subculture.

4. Education and Health

In trying to assess their quality of life, special
attention will be paid to the educational and health
problems affecting these communities. The nature and
extent of educational and health deficiencies prevailing in these communities and their relation to both
the quality of services available and the economic,
social and cultural nexus of these communities will be
examined. The extent to which the communities under
study are disadvantaged and underserved in respect of
educational and health services will be assessed.

5. Scope for Improvement

Finally, the broad inter-connections among
economic, social and cultural aspects of these communities and their relevance and implications for
programs seeking to improve the living conditions of
the urban poor will be considered.

THEORETICAL PERSPECTIVES

Systematic research on social and cultural
manifestations of urban poverty began with the **culture
of poverty** studies founded by Oscar Lewis in the
1950s. Lewis and his followers saw poverty not merely
as a lack of adequate income, but rather as a way of
life handed down from generation to generation through
well-defined social networks (Lewis 1959, 1965). This
theory holds that the uprooted slum dwellers, while
rejecting the dominant values of the larger society,
have certain values of their own, conditioned by their
upbringing, migration experience, economic circumstances, lifestyle and social segregation. Poor links with
the larger society, lack of collective organization,
weak family structures, personality features characterized by feelings of insecurity and dependence,
attitudes of resignation and fatalism and a lack of

concern for the future are among the features attributed to the culture of poverty.

The culture of poverty thesis started off a debate which, in a sense, is still continuing. The importance of beliefs, ideas and attitudes of the urban poor as a factor affecting and affected by their material circumstances is recognized by most contemporary observers. The examples of housing projects that deteriorate into slum conditions with the passage of time highlight the persistence of a way of life associated with poverty. However, a major weakness of this theory is its implicit assumption that the way of life of the urban poor is generated purely by conditions within their own communities. The structure of the larger society that determines and perpetuates the circumstances within the low-income communities is neglected in the culture of poverty studies. Further, this theory cannot explain the variation among different types of urban low-income communities. We can also question the validity of cross-cultural generalizations based on intensive anthropological studies in a limited number of small communities.

In the 1970s the **theory of marginality** emerged as a popular model for understanding the character of slums and shantytowns especially in Third World cities. These communities were considered marginal to the mainstream urban society in a geographical and spatial sense as well as in a social and economic sense (Adams 1974, Lomnitz 1977). Their spatially peripheral existence, lack of political power, weak connections with the center and poor representation in the industrial work force were seen as different aspects of marginality among the urban poor. Unlike the culture of poverty thesis, the theory of marginality enables us to conceptualize both internal and external conditions affecting the relevant communities.

7

While external circumstances give rise to their marginalization, the internal dynamics of these communities may be viewed as an adaption to, and at the same time, a reaction against conditions imposed by the larger society (Nelson 1969, Lomnitz 1977, Kapferer 1977). From the angle of adaptation, the recycling of urban waste through the intervention of shanty dwellers, the occupation of marginal land not suitable for other purposes, the economic organization of an informal sector (McGee 1971, Forbes 1981) and the development of social networks of reciprocal exchange as a system of mutual help are important features of these communities. On the other hand, urban unrest and riots, the high rate of crime and violence and the rejection of certain values of the larger society by the urban poor fall into proper perspective when seen as their reactions against the marginal position imposed upon them by the larger society. Certain observers have made a distinction between spatial and structural marginality and examined its implications for political action among the urban poor (Kapferer 1977).

While the theory of marginality may be seen as an improvement over the culture of poverty perspective, it too has certain limitations. The theory of marginality too does not take into account or explain variation among different types of urban low-income communities. Further, in so far as it does not explain how marginality may be overcome by the people concerned, it presents a static view of social reality (Perlman 1976).

J.F.C. Turner, in his conceptualization of the poor in Third World cities, describes them as a dynamic and potentially upwardly mobile category capable of and, at the same time, highly motivated towards improving themselves through their own efforts. Contrary to the images presented by culture of poverty and marginality theories, Turner argues that the **voluntary housing action** of the urban poor often constitutes a both rational and creative response on their part to their housing requirements (Turner 1967, 1970a, 1970b, 1977; Brett 1974).

Further, he contends that the housing requirements of the urban low-income families are not static but variable, depending on their length of stay in the city, security of employment and concern for status. For those newly arrived in the city, the first requirement of housing is that it be cheap and provides easy access to employment. Initially they are ready to sacrifice many of the comforts, security of tenure and status for the opportunity value of being present in the right place at the right time. Security of tenure and status value of their housing situation become important as they consolidate their position in urban society.

Turner identifies different types of urban settlements and places them in a continuum where levels of physical development vary from temporary shelter to middle-class housing. He argues against large scale housing construction by centralized agencies as it eliminates the freedom of the individuals concerned to determine their housing situation. Turner's ideas had a considerable influence on a recent shift of policy from slum clearance to slum upgrading evident in many Third World countries (Payne 1977). While this theory provides some insights into the housing action of the poor in Third World cities, by implication it tends to advocate a laissez-faire policy towards the urban poor. Further, it views the latter merely as home builders and, hence, its sociological significance is limited.

Finally, the **New Urban Sociology** founded by Castells re-examines many aspects of urban society using a Marxist perspective (Castells 1977, 1978, 1983). According to Castells, the urban centers in

capitalist societies are not only centers of production, distribution and consumption, but also important
centers of reproduction of a labor power responding to
the needs of a capitalist world system. Just as much
as the relevant production processes necessarily give
rise to contradictions between labor and capital, the
wider urban system concerned with the provision of
services essential for ensuring the reproduction of
labor power results in its own contradictions, usually
manifest in organized opposition to the state on the
part of the city dwellers. Castells argues that the
latter contradictions may be much sharper under
"dependent capitalism" in the Third World, where a
vast majority of shanty dwellers are deprived of an
access to basic urban services. This approach is much
useful for understanding contradictions in urban
society and the resulting unrest, protests and large
scale historical developments. However, up to now it
has had a limited applicability in the study of urban
communities and other such smaller social units
contained within urban society, particularly in the
Third World.

As will be seen, there is no one perspective
satisfactorily explaining all aspects of the communities studied. Therefore, the analytical framework
pursued here will be an essentially eclectic one.

URBAN POVERTY IN SRI LANKA: AN OVERVIEW

In contrast to the experience of many other
countries in the Third World, the rate of urbanization
in Sri Lanka has remained quite moderate over the past
several decades as evident from Table 1.1.

While the urban population in Sri Lanka, i.e. the
population living in areas administered by Town, Urban
or Municipal Councils, increased three-fold from 1.0
million in 1946 to 3.2 million in 1981, the share of
the urban population in the total population increased

only from 15.4 percent to 21.5 percent over this period of 35 years. The highest rate of urbanization was recorded for the period from 1953 to 1963. More recently there has been a sharp decrease in the rate of urbanization; between 1971 and 1981 the urban population increased at the rate of 1.21 percent per year as against the 4.23 percent annual increase recorded during the preceding intercensal period; the urban population in Sri Lanka grew at a rate lower than that of the total population in the country indicating that there has not been any significant rural-urban migration in Sri Lanka during this period.

TABLE 1.1

GROWTH OF URBAN POPULATION IN SRI LANKA, 1946 TO 1981

Census Year	Urban Population	Urban Population as a % of Total Pop.	Average Annual Increase (%)	
			Total Population	Urban Population
1946	1,023,042	15.4	1.52	2.20
1953	1,239,133	15.3	1.84	2.77
1963	2,016,285	19.1	2.65	4.88
1971	2,848,116	22.4	2.20	4.23
1981	3,192,489	21.5	1.67	1.21

Source: Census Reports

It is important to note that the findings of the 1981 census do not indicate any unprecedented urban growth in Sri Lanka since 1977, despite liberalized economic policies implemented since that year and the accompanying measures such as urban development and the establishment of a Free Trade Zone (FTZ).

11

TABLE 1.2

DISTRIBUTION OF URBAN POPULATION BY TYPE OF URBAN
AREA, 1963 TO 1981

| | Census Year | | |
	1963	1971	1981
No. of Units			
Municipal Councils	10	12	12
Urban Councils	35	37	39
Town Councils	54	86	83
Total	99	135	134
Population			
Municipal Councils	1,032,000	1,220,000	1,305,000
Urban Councils	581,000	771,000	898,000
Town Councils	403,000	857,000	989,000
Total	2,016,000	2,848,000	3,192,000
% of Total Urban Population			
Municipal Councils	51.2	42.8	40.9
Urban Councils	28.8	27.1	28.1
Town Councils	20.0	30.1	31.0
Total	100.0	100.0	100.0

Some important features of the urbanization
process in Sri Lanka from 1963 to 1981 are evident in
Table 1.2. One significant finding is that while the
share of the total urban population living in
Municipal Council areas declined from 51.2 percent in
1963 to 40.9 percent in 1981, that of Town Council
areas increased from 20 percent in 1963 to 31 percent
in 1981. It is evident that while the number of
Municipal and Urban Councils remained relatively

12

stable throughout the period under review, the number
of Town Councils increased from 54 in 1963 to 86 in
1971. It has been pointed out that the re-
classification of urban areas and the resulting
increase in the number of Town Councils is the single
most important factor responsible for the unusually
high rates of urbanization witnessed in the 1953-1971
period [1] (see also Table 1.1). Some of the previous
research also point to the growth of small towns,
especially in new settlement areas, as an important
and in some ways a unique feature of the urbanization
process in Sri Lanka (see Abeysekera 1980).

TABLE 1.3

ANNUAL POPULATION GROWTH, 1946 TO 1981

Area	Percentage Annual Increase			
	1946-53	1953-63	1963-71	1971-81
CMC Area	2.4	1.9	1.2	0.5
Colombo Suburbs	4.5	3.4	3.7	1.8
Colombo District	3.4	2.7	2.7	1.3
Sri Lanka (Urban)	2.8	4.9	4.2	1.2

Source: Census Reports

An analysis of the urban growth in Colombo, the
primate city of Sri Lanka, is given in Table 1.3. It
shows that there is a progressive decline in the rate
of population growth in the Colombo Municipal Council

13

(CMC) area as well as in the Colombo district as a whole between 1946 and 1981. During the 1971-81 period, the rate of urban growth slowed down in Colombo, its suburbs as well as in the Colombo district as a whole when compared to the preceding intercensal period [2]. During the 1971-81 period, the rate of population growth in the CMC area was much lower than that in urban Sri Lanka as a whole. Only Colombo suburbs, including Dehiwala-Mt. Lavinia Municipal Council area and Moratuwa and Seeduwa-Katunayake Urban Council areas, recorded any significant population growth during the period under review.

In interpreting the data reported so far we must bear in mind that the definition of urban areas on the basis of the type of local government entity serving a given area is somewhat arbitrary and that the urban sprawl may often spill over the designated urban areas. Further, an unknown number of people who commute daily to work in Colombo and other towns from the surrounding areas is not taken into account in census figures on urban growth. In view of these circumstances the census reports consistently note that it is difficult to draw a sharp distinction between urban and rural areas in the case of Sri Lanka. While these considerations cannot be overlooked, it is nevertheless evident that the rural-oriented policies followed by successive governments in Sri Lanka along with successful population control measures have so far averted any large scale rural-urban migration in the country. However, once the limit of rural resettlement programs is reached, the pace of urbanization in the country may gradually increase in time to come.

Despite the slow pace of urbanization in Sri Lanka up to now, the available data indicate that the problem of urban poverty is quite acute in Sri Lanka. This is evident from various reports on income dis-

14

TABLE 1.4

INCOME DISTRIBUTION IN SRI LANKA BY SECTORS 1973, 1978/79 AND 1981/82

Ranked Income Receivers	Year(s)	Percentage of Total Income				
		Urban	Rural	Estate	All Island	
Lowest 20%	1973	5.39	3.35	7.51	4.97	
	1978/79	3.34	3.49	7.73	3.76	
	1981/82	3.57	3.71	8.24	3.70	
Second 20%	1973	10.74	11.60	11.73	10.08	
	1978/79	8.49	8.60	13.21	8.36	
	1981/82	7.66	8.78	12.63	8.08	
Third 20%	1973	16.13	16.95	14.90	15.85	
	1978/79	13.24	14.11	16.76	13.22	
	1981/82	11.63	13.50	16.51	12.50	
Fourth 20%	1973	22.42	23.39	20.65	23.21	
	1978/79	19.26	20.82	22.22	20.35	
	1981/82	18.15	19.90	21.65	19.20	
Highest 20%	1973	45.32	42.71	45.21	45.89	
	1978/79	55.67	52.98	40.08	54.31	
	1981/82	58.99	54.11	40.97	56.52	
Median Monthly Income	1973	255.00	197.00	88.00	180.00	
	1978/79	539.00	429.00	252.00	408.00	
	1981/82	977.00	781.00	376.00	612.00	

Source: Consumer Finances Surveys, 1973, 1978/79 and 1981/82

tribution in urban areas (see Table 1.4). Even though
the median monthly income per income earner in the
urban sector has rapidly increased over time, income
disparities between the lowest and the highest income
groups have worsened during the 1973-82 period.
Whereas the lowest 40 percent of income earners in the
urban sector received 16.1 percent of total income in
1973, it declined to 11.8 in 1978/79 and 11.2 in
1981/82.

In contrast, the share of the highest 20 percent
of income earners proportionately increased from 45.3
percent of the total income in 1973 to 55.7 percent in
1978/79 and nearly 59 percent in 1981/82. Thus by
1981/82, while the lowest 40 percent of the urban
income earners received only 11 percent of the total
income in the urban sector, the highest 20 percent of
the income earners in the urban sector received nearly
60 percent of the total urban income.

The analysis of the degree of income inequality in
various sectors of the Sri Lanka economy using the
Gini Coefficient shows that of the three sectors of
the Sri Lanka economy the urban sector has consistently recorded the highest degree of income inequality in
three successive nationwide surveys conducted between
1973 and 1982 (see Table 1.5). Further, the degree of
income inequality in the urban sector, as indicated by
the Gini Coefficient, has progressively increased from
0.4 to 0.54 between 1973 and 1982. Parallel nationwide
surveys conducted by the Department of Census and
Statistics confirm the above findings [3].

Thus the urbanization experience of Sri Lanka
since independence can be characterized as one where
a slow rate of urbanization has been accompanied by a
progressive income differentiation within the urban
society.

TABLE 1.5

GINI COEFFICIENT BASED ON MONTHLY INCOME OF INCOME
EARNERS IN SRI LANKA BY SECTORS, 1973, 1978/79 AND
1981/82

Sector	Gini Coefficient		
	1973	1978/79	1981/82
Urban	0.40	0.51	0.54
Rural	0.37	0.49	0.49
Estate	0.37	0.32	0.32
All Island	0.41	0.49	0.52

Source: Consumer Finance Surveys, Central Bank, 1973,
        1978/79 and 1981/82

The processes noted in the preceding paragraphs
have given rise to the formation of a variety of
low-income communities in Colombo and several other
cities in Sri Lanka. For the most part, the variation
among these communities as well as their distinction
from the larger urban society are defined according to
their housing and neighborhood characteristics. In
Colombo city, three types of low-income communities
have been identified for various purposes. They are
referred to as Tenement Gardens, Slum Gardens and
Shanty Communities. The housing condition in all three
types of communities is officially described as
"substandard". The specific features of each type of
community are as follows.

Tenement Gardens

These are old-established working-class neighborhoods situated in inner-city areas. Each Tenement

17

Garden invariably comprises of compactly arranged rows
of tenement houses which are over 50 years old. They
were built by enterprising businessmen in colonial
society, mostly during the period from 1880 to 1930 as
rental accommodation for port workers, factory workers
and other categories of urban workers of the time.
Both the housing and public utilities in the Tenement
Gardens deteriorated over time due to structural
defects, poor maintenance, overuse and tenurial
problems.

Slum Gardens

The Slum Gardens consist of old deteriorating
houses other than tenements. The history of these
neighborhoods too, can often be traced back to the
colonial period. They too are usually found in inner-
city areas. Unlike the Tenement Gardens, the Slum
Gardens evolved from original residential areas
occupied by the affluent in the city. As the latter
gradually moved to newly-established fashionable
suburban areas such as Cinnamon Gardens, their former
residences in inner-city areas were rapidly converted
into working-class rental housing by various
categories of housing intermediaries. The physical
conditions in these neighborhoods too gradually
deteriorated over time due to increased density,
neglect and other such factors. Both the construction
of tenements and conversion of old residential areas
into working-class neighborhoods took place prior to
the formulation of a Building Code by the
Municipality; hence no official building standards
guided the construction of these working-class
accommodations.

Shanty Communities

The shanty communities differ in many respects
from the older working-class neighborhoods described
above. Unlike the two types of inner-city neighbor-

hoods which may be commonly referred to as slums, the shanty communities mostly evolved since 1948 so as to accommodate excess population from slum areas as well as several kinds of new arrivals in the city. In terms of location, these communities radiate along canals, river banks, sea coast, railway lines and roadside with their heaviest concentration in the outskirts of the city (see Map 2).

Often the shanty dwellers are squatters on previously unused marginal land owned by the government, municipality or private landlords, whether they are road reservations, river or canal banks or low-lying areas subject to periodic monsoonal floods. In contrast to the slum buildings invariably made of durable building materials, the shanties have been hurriedly built using locally available temporary building materials, including cadjan (woven coconut leaves), wooden planks, tin, cardboard and other such industrial waste. While there is a minimum of municipal services legally provided in the slums, the shanty dwellers, who are regarded as unauthorized residents of the city, were until recently only partially accommodated through public latrines and common water taps installed in nearby public places.

In Colombo and certain other cities in Sri Lanka a well defined neighborhood inhabited exclusively by the poor - whether it is a Tenement Garden, Slum Garden or a shanty community - is commonly referred to as a "watta" (lit. estate). The origin of the term is not clear, but perhaps it signified the fact that at the outset each low-income neighborhood was an undivided property unit owned, administered or controlled by a single person. Their original subordination to a single landlord or his agent is often implied by the names of these communities, e.g. Asnarge Watta (Asnar's block), Postmasterge Watta (Post Master's block), Nommara Tune Watta (No.3 block). At other times the names of the communities refer to a particular economic activity, e.g. Maswatta (beef producers' area), Keselwatta (banana garden).

In some official documents as well as in some recent literature on the subject, the term "watta" is rendered into English as "garden" (see Adamson 1982). This, however, is inappropriate as the term "watta" is used in the particular context more in the sense of a "housing estate". In order to avoid confusion, this report will consistently use the Sinhala term "watta" as a generic term for urban low-income communities in Sri Lanka. Unlike terms such as "slum" or "shanty community", the term "watta" is by and large free of any derogatory connotations [4]. Finally, the term "watta" is acceptable to and indeed used by the watta-dwellers themselves.

TABLE 1.6

DISTRIBUTION OF LOW-INCOME POPULATION IN COLOMBO CITY
BY TYPE OF NEIGHBORHOOD, 1974

Type of Neighborhood	No. of Houses	No. of Families	Population	%
Tenement	20,507	24,623	123,115	45.3
Slum Garden	8,207	9,840	48,907	18.0
Shanty	16,250	19,953	99,645	36.7
Total	44,964	54,416	271,667	100.0

Source: CMC Administration Report, 1974

The total number of watta communities in the CMC area is estimated to be in the region of 1,200 to 1,500 [5]. Table 1.6 gives the distribution of the population in various types of low-income communities in Colombo city.

20

As of 1974, the largest share of the low-income population in Colombo city was in Tenement Gardens, followed by the shanty communities and Slum Gardens.

Precise data regarding the growth of different types of low-income communities in Colombo city are not available. On the whole it appears that while the number of shanty communities, i.e., Tenement and Slum Gardens, remained more or less stable after 1950 or so, there has been a considerable growth in the number of shanty communities particularly in the 1950s and 1960s (see Table 1.7).

TABLE 1.7

ESTIMATED NUMBER OF SHANTY UNITS IN COLOMBO CITY

Year	No. of Shanty Units	Source
1953	1,347	CMC
1960	13,332	CMC
1974	16,250	CMC
1979	15,951	UDA

According to Table 1.7, the number of shanty units in Colombo city sharply increased between 1953 and 1960 [6]. The UDA estimates for 1979 indicate a slight reduction in the number of shanty units after 1974, but the more recent trends in regard to shanty growth in Colombo are not known at present.

Information regarding the size of watta communities in Colombo city is presented in Table 1.8. Thus the average community size is about 35 households with an estimated total population of 210. Hence an average watta community is quite small in size.

TABLE 1.8

DISTRIBUTION OF A SAMPLE OF WATTA COMMUNITIES IN
COLOMBO ACCORDING TO THEIR SIZE

No. of Households	No. of Watta Communities	Percentage of the total
Under 25	127	49
26 - 50	76	29
51 - 75	31	12
76 - 100	8	3
Over 100	18	7
Total	260	100

Average = 35.3
Standard deviation = 29
Source: Tilakaratna et al. 1984, p. 14

As for the provincial pattern of urbanization a
number of provincial towns including Ratnapura, Nuwara
Eliya, Batticaloa and Jaffna recorded a faster rate of
growth compared to Colombo during the 1971-81 period.
Many of the provincial towns too have distinct low-
income neighborhoods which may be broadly distinguished as slums and shanty areas. For instance, in Kandy
town with a total population of 97,872 in 1981, the
Kandy Municipal Council (KMC) had identified a total
of 45 low-income localities with an estimated total
population of 10,000. Several of these communities
were locally referred to as watta.

A special type of low-income communities found
mostly in Kandy and other hill country towns is known
as "labor lines". Like their counterparts in the
estates, these urban communities originated in the
colonial era as working-class neighborhoods occupied
exclusively by the immigrant Indian Tamil workers. In

22

the case of these urban "labor lines", their inhabitants (both men and women) have always been employed by the local Municipal or Urban Councils as street sweepers and sanitary laborers. These communities have evolved as outcast ethnic enclaves functionally connected with city administration, but politically, socially and culturally cut-off from the mainstream urban society.

Thus on the whole there are well defined low-income neighborhoods both in Colombo and provincial towns.

Slum and Shanty Upgrading

The latest official response to the problem of urban poverty in Sri Lanka consists mainly of a comprehensive program of slum and shanty upgrading implemented since 1978 by various agencies under the Ministry of Local Government, Housing and Construction with the assistance of UNICEF, UNDP and several other international organizations and NGOs.

As the earlier governmental efforts at direct construction of low-cost housing for the benefit of the urban poor and the accompanying programs of slum clearance were found to be too costly, socially disruptive and not effective in solving the housing problem of a vast majority of the expanding slum and shanty population, the relevant agencies of the government turned to a new strategy involving the planned upgrading of the existing housing stock among the urban poor. Encouraged by the success of several pilot projects started by the Colombo Master Plan Project (CMPP), the Slum and Shanty Division of the UDA established in 1978 began a comprehensive program of slum and shanty upgrading in selected locations in Colombo and other towns. These projects involved the installation of common amenities like new water taps, improved latrines, bathrooms and waste disposal

23

facilities and construction of paved footpaths, drains, etc. in the relevant communities together with regularization of plots and renovation or new construction of houses where necessary.

Parallel to the efforts of the UDA, a separate program for improving environmental sanitation and related community development activities covering a total slum and shanty population of 80,000 distributed in 250 communities was begun in 1979 through the collaboration of UNICEF, CMC and the CAB. In 1985 the Slum and Shanty Division was transferred from UDA to the NHDA and, as a result, the slum and shanty upgrading program inclusive of the joint UNICEF-CMC-CAB operations became integrated with the Million Houses Program led by the then Prime Minister of Sri Lanka [7]. This has led to the development of a nationwide Urban Housing Sub-Program under which a coordinated effort is made to settle land issues hindering housing improvements and provide required infrastructural facilities together with low-interest loans for housing improvements for the benefit of the urban poor.

The studies conducted by UDA in 1978 and 1979 determined "upgradable" slums and shanties in Colombo city. All slums and shanties excluding the following were considered suitable for upgrading (UDA 1979: 9-10).

1. Locations liable to serious flooding.

2. Locations unsafe for human habitation and locations where provision of sewage disposal and other services is rendered impossible due to one factor or another.
3. Locations needed for priority alternative uses, including construction of roads and other public utilities.

24

4. Subdivided slum tenements where upgrading is technically unfeasible.

On the basis of the above factors the UDA estimated that 80 percent of all slums and 59 percent of all shanty neighborhoods in the Colombo city are upgradable. Those not suitable for upgrading were to be relocated in stages.

A systematic assessment of the progress and achievements of the Slum and Shanty Upgrading Program has not been made up to now. A UDA statement issued in November 1982 noted that up to that date a total of 20,000 slum dwellings and 17,500 shanty dwellings, comprising about 15 percent of the total slum and shanty population in Colombo city had been upgraded (UDA 1982). Since then the program has expanded to other areas of Colombo and other cities in Sri Lanka. According to the staff of the NHDA, as of July 1987 the program covered as much as 75 percent of the Tenement Gardens in Colombo. The number of shanty neighborhoods affected by the program up to July 1987 was reported to be much less. The data concerning the progress of the program in provincial towns were scanty.

On the whole the available data indicate that housing and infrastructural facilities in a substantial number of slum neighborhoods mostly in Colombo have been upgraded as of 1987. The overall impact of this program must be carefully assessed through future research. Among the important topics for research are: the proportion of the urban poor in each city benefited by this program; the success in recovery of loans; how far the upgraded facilities are sustained over time; and the extent to which the upgraded facilities continue to serve the original target group.

The scope of the present study does not include any assessment of the slum and shanty upgrading program now being implemented in Sri Lanka.

REVIEW OF LITERATURE ON THE URBAN POOR IN SRI LANKA

There is a considerable amount of published and unpublished work relating to urban poverty in Sri Lanka. Detailed listing or review of such work can be found in Kandiah (1975), Mendis and Ranbanda (1983) and Mendis and Rubasingham (1982). The unpublished work consists mainly of work under the Colombo Master Plan Project, reports in CMC, UDA and NHDA and dissertation work, especially at University of Moratuwa. Much of the recent literature relating to the subject focuses on two ongoing projects in the urban sector, namely Slum and Shanty Upgrading under UDA and NHDA and the UNICEF-CMC-CAB Project on Environmental Health and Community Development. The existing literature dealing with the urban poor in Sri Lanka can be grouped under the following topics:

1. Housing and Urban Development
2. Health
3. Demographic Aspects
4. Informal Sector
5. Community Development
6. Social Aspects

We will briefly examine what we consider the most important work under the above topics.

Housing and Urban Development

Considerable attention has been focused on slum and shanty housing and the accompanying physical characteristics. Questions regarding utilization of space, density and architectural features of slum and shanty dwelling units have been raised by Lankatilake (1976) and De Tissera and Ganesan (1978). Several

26

studies, including a Marga study (1976), made efforts to assess the housing needs of the urban poor. The question of upgrading of slum and shanty housing has been examined in several studies including CMPP (1977, 1978), Lankatilake (1976) and Karunatilleke (1978). The program of slum and shanty upgrading under UDA and NHDA and its impact have been examined by Rodell (1980), Steinberg (1982, 1983) and Selvarajah (1983).

The above studies describe the housing problems affecting the urban poor. They emphasize the physical aspects of slum and shanty existence. Slum and shanty upgrading primarily involves an effort to improve the quality of the physical environment in these neighborhoods, but the effects of such effort will be limited unless they are accompanied by appropriate community development measures. People's orientation to housing, connections between housing and employment and those between housing and level of social organization are not adequately covered in any of the above studies.

Health

An important contribution to the understanding of the health status of the urban poor in Colombo comes from a report prepared by the Marga Institute (1982). This report is based on a sample survey of 660 households distributed in some 27 slum and shanty communities. It has information relating to immunization coverage, breast feeding, family planning, morbidity, contact with public health staff and other such issues relevant to urban primary health care programs.

In addition to such city-wide surveys, more intensive community studies are needed for understanding the socio-cultural and ecological context of health and disease as related to urban poverty. Community variations in regard to health must also be explored. A beginning for such more intensive urban health studies has been made by Silva (1986).

Demographic Aspects

Several studies focus on population growth and rural-urban migration as related to the slum and shanty formation in Sri Lanka. Included in this category are studies by Gunatilake (1973), Kurukulasuriya (1979), Karunatilleke (1979) and Karunatilake (1981). These studies show that even though the rate of urbanization in Sri Lanka has remained quite low since 1948, shanty formation has been an important aspect of city expansion. The post-1977 trends in rural-urban migration are not covered by any existing literature. The demographic trends within the slum and shanty communities though noted by some authors (e.g. Perera 1973, Dias 1976), have not been studied carefully.

Informal Sector

There has been a considerable amount of work concerning the role of the informal sector in urban Sri Lanka. A pioneering study by the Marga Institute (1979a: 27) estimated that nearly 20 percent of the total working population in the Colombo city is employed in the informal sector. Based on a sample survey of 1,200 informal sector enterprises in Colombo city, the Marga study examined the internal organization of the informal sector, its links with the formal sector, characteristics of the informal sector workers and the ways in which their conditions may be improved (see also Casinader & Ellepola 1979). It appears that this Marga study did not cover a whole range of illegal operations, including prostitution, gambling, manufacturing and distribution of illicit liquor etc., which too could be included in the informal sector. Therefore, it is quite possible that the actual number of informal-sector workers in Colombo city is much

28

higher than the number estimated by the Marga study. Further, the connections between the informal sector and the distribution of slum and shanty communities were not examined.

The environmental impact of the informal sector with special reference to its effects on waste disposal, traffic congestion and use of public utilities was examined in a subsequent study (see Bandusena 1983). In their treatment of the subject Perera (1979, 1981, 1983) and Vidanagamachchi (1981) highlighted the limitations of the informal sector concept when applied to concrete examples of urban economic activities.

Community Development

There are several reports on community development efforts in urban Sri lanka. Mendis (1976) and Radampola and Selvarajah (1977) describe some spontaneous community efforts in selected wattas in Colombo. Much of the recent literature on the subject relates to the experiences of the UNICEF/CMC/CAB Project on Environmental Health and Community Development referred to earlier (Adamson 1982, Cassim et al. 1982, Karunaratne 1982, UNICEF 1983, Tilakaratna et al. 1984). This project involves the provision of physical amenities, health education, PHC activities, creation of a cadre of community workers called "health wardens" and establishment of community organizations in selected wattas in Colombo. As reported in detail by Tilakaratna et al. (1984), the project has achieved varying degrees of success as regards its various objectives. On the whole the results indicate that the successful creation of viable community organizations is more difficult to achieve than the mere installation of physical amenities in these communities. This project has the merit of giving equal emphasis on physical improvement and community development. It also involves intersectoral collaboration. The future research should focus on its cost-effectiveness, long term viability and broader impact on community life (Chandrasiri 1982).

Social Aspects

On the whole, relative to the physical conditions in slum and shanty communities, their social aspects have received insufficient attention in the existing literature. The few studies available on social aspects of these communities are rather sketchy and remain unrelated to one another. The early studies covering social aspects by and large focused on manifestations of social disorganization, including neglect of children (Jayasooriya 1955), juvenile delinquency (Jayasooriya & Kariyawasam 1958), crime (Tambiah 1957) and prostitution (Silva 1985).

In an early account Mendis (1977) briefly characterized the social organization of squatter settlements but his arguments were not based on an intensive ethnographic research in any actual community. Bulankulame et al. (1977), based on a sample survey of households, describe the poor integration of squatters into the mainstream urban life in Sri Lanka. However, Kapferer (1977) found that compared to their counterparts in African cities, the shanty dwellers in Sri Lanka are less marginal since caste-based political loyalties and patronage links remain important among the latter. Ariyaratne (1979) noted the predominance of minority ethnic groups, especially Muslims, in the inner-city slums in Colombo.

The present study seeks to supplement the existing work on the urban poor by providing a more comprehensive account of social life in four selected urban low-income communities in Sri Lanka. In contrast to many of the earlier studies, it uses the ethnographic method for obtaining reliable qualitative data concerning several related aspects of the communities studied. While the existing studies on the urban poor in Sri Lanka are by and large Colombo centered, the present study deals with a total of four communities, two from Colombo and two from provincial towns, in order to understand broad variations among the relevant communities in Sri Lanka.

Finally, unlike many of the previous studies the present study does not seek to evaluate the effects of any specific intervention program like slum and shanty upgrading; rather our aim is to examine a sample of urban low-income communities in Sri Lanka in their normal socio-economic settings.

METHODOLOGY OF THE STUDY

The data reported here were obtained through intensive field research in four selected urban low-income communities in Sri Lanka. Detailed ethnographic research was conducted in two communities in Colombo, one in Kandy and one in Negombo. The four communities studied were Jude Mawatha and Swarna Mawatha in Colombo, Soyza Lane in Kandy (prior to its relocation in another part of the city in 1986) and Kamachchode in Negombo [8]. The first and third communities were inner-city slums while the second was a shanty community. The fourth community, Kamachchode, had a mixed character as it consisted of more or less equal numbers of slum type and shanty type dwelling units.

The communities studied were purposively chosen with operational considerations mainly influencing their choice. An effort was made to include a range of urban low-income communities distributed in Sri Lankan cities of varied sizes [9]. Under the supervision of the Principal Investigators (PIs), a trained male sociology graduate conducted ethnographic field research in each of the four communities studied for a period of six to nine months from 1983 to 1984. They recorded in field notebooks their daily observations concerning various aspects of community life. The two PIs monitored the data collection procedure by reading the relevant entries in the field notebooks every fortnight and instructing the field assistants as to what they should look for in the weeks ahead.

The qualitative data obtained through the above procedure was supplemented by the administration of a 22-paged structured questionnaire covering a variety of topics, including migration history, basic household data, employment, income and expenditure, health, community organization, literacy, recreational activities and attitudes. This household census covered all households willing to respond to the questionnaire in each community. Finally, informal discussions were held with the staff of UDA and NHDA, relevant community leaders and municipal administrators in each city included in this study.

DEFINITION OF TERMS

1. Slum

An inner-city neighborhood characterized by high density and housing units that are deteriorated permanent structures.

2. Shanty neighborhood

A densely populated urban or peri-urban neighborhood characterized mainly by small housing units made from non-durable materials including recycled urban waste.

3. Watta

A slum, a cluster of shanties, or any other poor neighborhood found in an urban area in Sri Lanka.

4. Social Organization

The orderly social framework within which members of a given social group interact with one another.

5. Culture

The way of life and pattern of thinking characteristic of a given social group.

6. Community

A group of people who frequently interact with one another by virtue of sharing a common neighborhood.

NOTES

1. Census of Population and Housing 1981: General Report, Vol.3, p.68.

2. It must be noted here that the area covered by the Colombo district became reduced between 1971 and 1981 due to the creation of the new district of Gampaha. This partly accounts for the reported drop in population growth in the Colombo district during the period under review. This change of district boundaries, however, did not affect the CMC area.

3. For details see Labor Force and Socio-Economic Survey, Sri Lanka, 1980/81; Household Income and Expenditure. Colombo, Dept. of Census and Statistics, 1983.

4. For the same reason certain derogatory local terms used in reference to these neighborhoods such as "Koriyawa", "Colony", "Labor Lines" etc. will be avoided in the present account.

5. See Adamson 1982 and UDA 1979.

33

6. The rapid growth of shanties between 1953 and 1960 has been attributed to a relatively lenient attitude adopted towards urban squatters by the relevant urban authorities at the time.

7. For details see Siriwardena 1985.

8. The actual names of the communities studied are used in this monograph. Where names of individuals are mentioned fictitious names are used so as to conceal their identity.

9. However, the authors do not claim that this study covers the full range of urban low-income communities in Sri Lanka.

CHAPTER TWO

SETTING

This chapter presents basic information about the four communities covered by the study. Map 1 shows the distribution of the major urban centers in Sri Lanka, including Colombo, Kandy and Negombo, relevant to the present study. In the description that follows, the study communities in Colombo, Kandy and Negombo are introduced in that order.

JUDE MAWATHA

This community is situated in the northern tip of Colombo, a predominantly low-income area in the city (see Map 2). The community is named after St. Jude's Mawatha, a by-lane that serves as the main access to the community (see Map 4). The community is included in Ward No. 44 of the CMC and the Colombo North electorate of the National State Assembly. This area, in the northern tip of the city of Colombo, was at the turn of the century a prime residential area, occupied by the city elite. Subsequently the rich moved to new suburban areas in the southern parts of the city. As the well-to-do families moved southward, Colombo North and Colombo Central gradually deteriorated into a working-class residential area characterized by poor housing, congestion and a run-down atmosphere. Thus in terms of historical background and neighborhood characteristics, the Jude Mawatha community broadly comes under the Slum Garden type described in Chapter One.

35

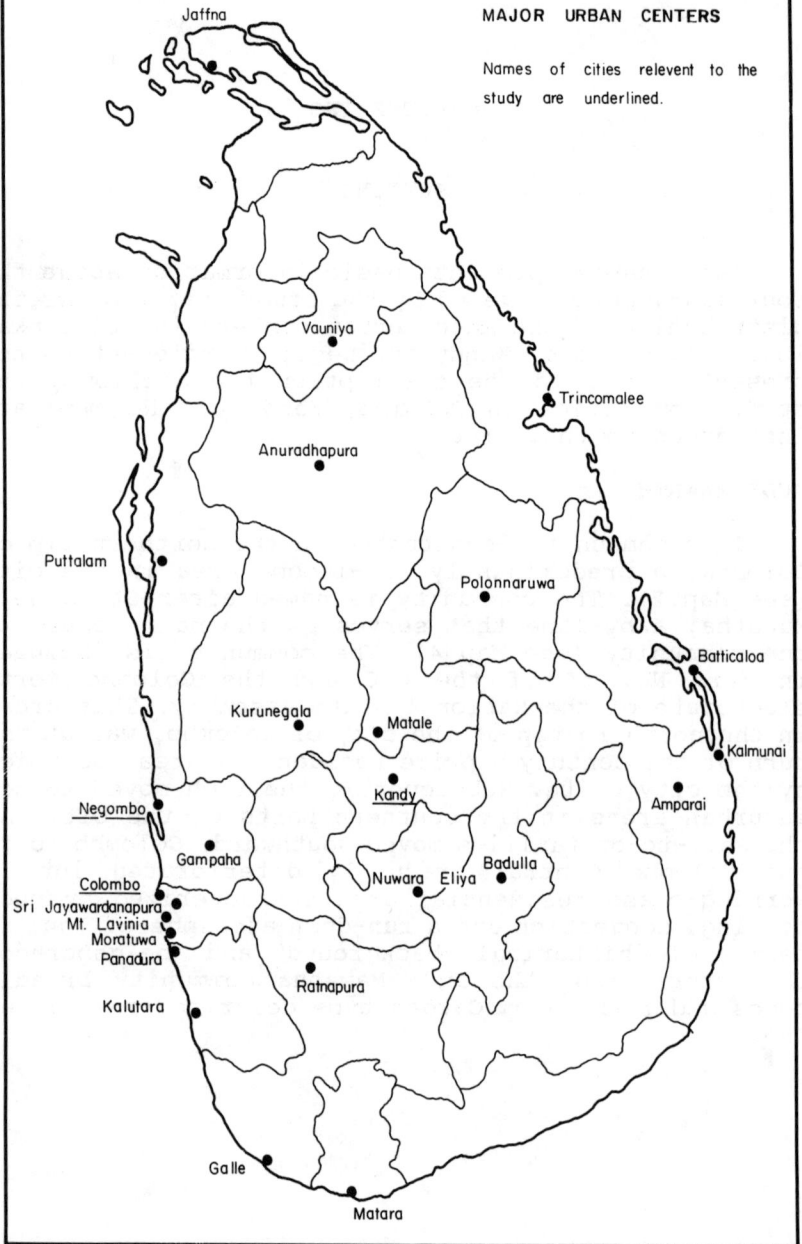

Map I : **MAP OF SRI LANKA SHOWING MAJOR URBAN CENTERS**

Names of cities relevent to the study are underlined.

Jaffna

Vauniya

Trincomalee

Anuradhapura

Puttalam

Polonnaruwa

Batticaloa

Kurunegala

Matale

Kalmunai

Negombo

Kandy

Amparai

Gampaha

Nuwara Eliya   Badulla

Colombo
Sri Jayawardanapura
Mt. Lavinia
Moratuwa
Panadura

Ratnapura

Kalutara

Galle

Matara

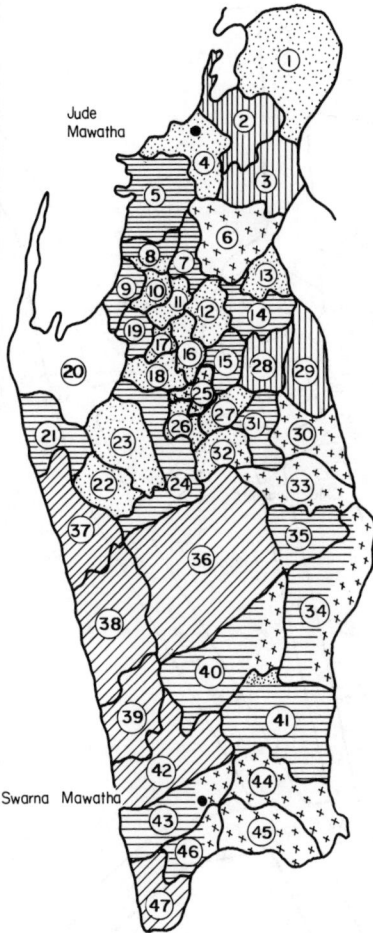

Map **2** : **HOUSING PATTERN** : **CITY OF COLOMBO**

LIST OF WARDS

1. Mattakkuliya
2. Modera
3. Mahawatta
4. Aluthmawatha
5. Lunupokuna
6. Bloemendhal
7. Kotahena East
8. Kotahena West
9. Kochchikade North
10. Ginthupitiya
11. Masangasvidiya
12. New Bazaar
13. Grandpass North
14. Grandpass South
15. Maligawatta West
16. Aluthkade East
17. Aluthkade West
18. Kehelwatta
19. Kochchikade
20. Fort
21. Kompannavidiya
22. Wekanda
23. Hunupitiya
24. Suduwella
25. Panchikawatta
26. Maradana
27. Maligakanda
28. Maligawatta East
29. Dematagoda
30. Wanathamulla
31. Kuppiyawatta East
32. Kuppiyawatta West
33. Borella North
34. Narahenpita
35. Borella South
36. Cinnaman Gardens
37. Kollupitiya
38. Bambalapitiya
39. Milagiriya
40. Thimbirigasyaya
41. Kirula
42. Havelock Town
43. Wellawatta North
44. Kirullapane
45. Pamankada East
46. Pamankada West
47. Pamankada South

LEGEND

Slum		Middle Class	
Shanty		Upper Class	
Slum - Shanty mix		Office & Shop Buildings	

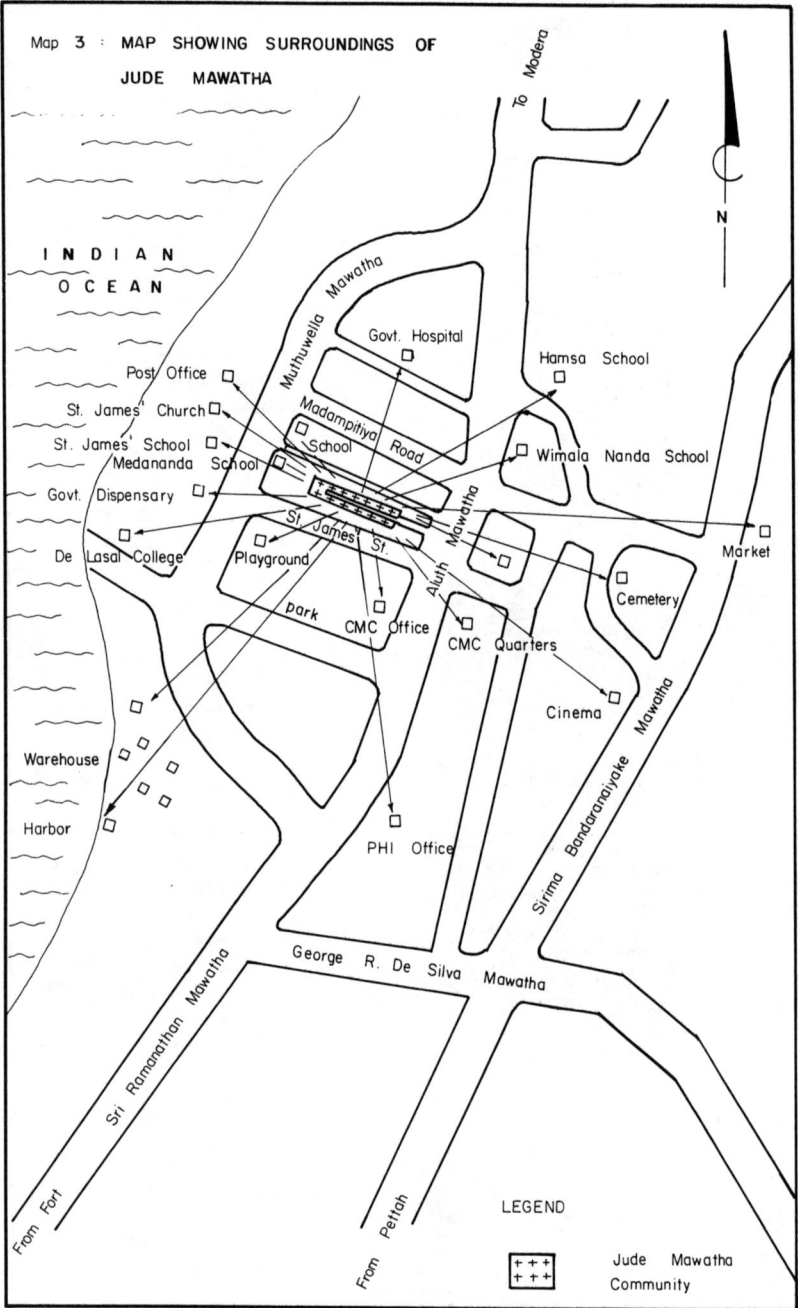

Map 3 : MAP SHOWING SURROUNDINGS OF JUDE MAWATHA

INDIAN OCEAN

To Modera

N

Muthuwella Mawatha

Govt. Hospital

Hamsa School

Post Office

St. James' Church

St. James' School

Medananda School

Madampitiya Road

School

Wimala Nanda School

Govt. Dispensary

De Lasal College

Playground

St. James St.

Auth Mawatha

Market

Cemetery

park

CMC Office

CMC Quarters

Cinema

Sirima Bandaranaiyake Mawatha

Warehouse

Harbor

PHI Office

Sri Ramanathan Mawatha

George R. De Silva Mawatha

From Fort

From Pettah

LEGEND

| + + + |
| + + + |

Jude Mawatha Community

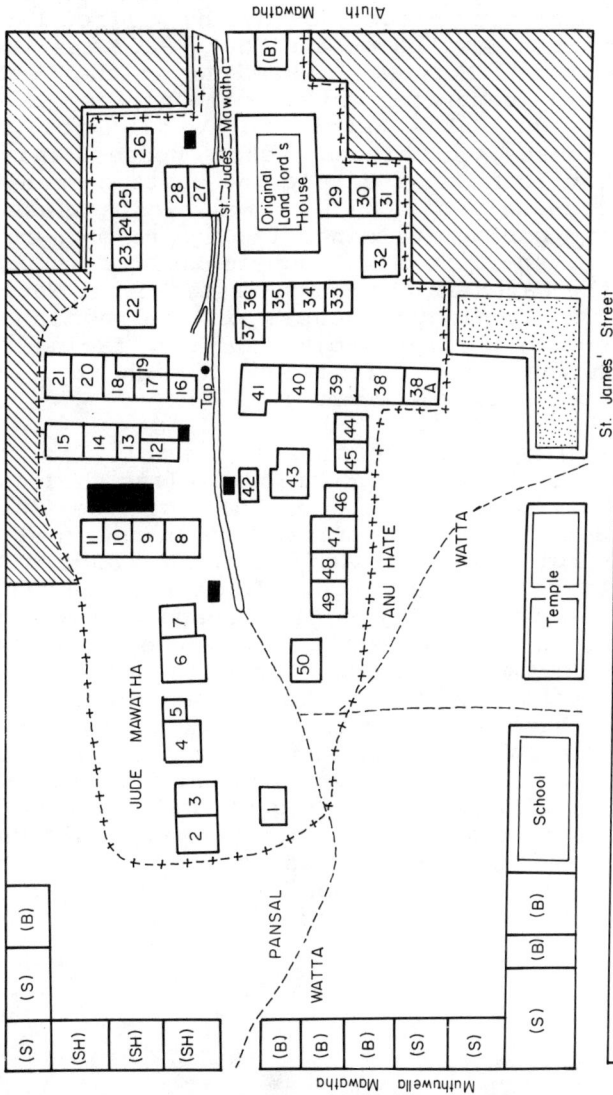

Map 4 : JUDE MAWATHA COMMUNITY MAP

LEGEND :

- + - Watta boundary
- - - - Footpath
- ── Drain
(B) Boutique
(S) Shop
(SH) Shop house
Middle Class Houses
Middle Class Flats
Common Toilet
Storeyed Building
• Common water Tap

St. Jude's Mawatha lies off Aluth Mawatha Road
which connects Modera and Mattakkuliya in the extreme
North of the city to commercial centers of Fort and
Pettah (see Map 3 and 4). As a narrow by-lane, St.
Jude's Mawatha connects Muthuwella Mawatha on the West
and Aluth Mawatha on the East. As seen in Map 4 in a
rectangular city block, bounded by Wilfred Lane on the
North, Aluth Mawatha on the East, St.James' Street on
the South and Muthuwella Mawatha on the West, there
are three separate watta communities, i.e. Jude
Mawatha, Anu Hathe Watta and Pansal Watta, middle-
class houses, boutiques, shop houses and certain
public buildings. As a rule the watta communities are
inconspicuously situated behind middle-class houses,
shops and public buildings facing the main roads. For
instance, the Jude Mawatha neighborhood is bounded by
Anu Hathe Watta in the South-West, Pansal Watta on the
West, the low-income houses of Wilfred Lane in the
North-West and middle-class houses facing the main
road in the other directions. A high wall separates
the latter from the community.

The main entrance to the community is through a
narrow passage between middle-class houses and a
boutique. Approximately a half of the St. Jude's
Mawatha is tarred. It turns into an untarred footpath
at the Muthuwella Mawatha end. St. Jude's Mawatha,
first tarred 50 years ago, slopes up, away from Aluth
Mawatha thus forming a higher and a lower section.
Even though all houses along St. Jude's Mawatha belong
to the low-income group, there is some variation in
house types. Most of the houses closer to Aluth
Mawatha have brick walls, tiled roofs and lattice
fronts. Further on in Jude Mawatha, the houses are
made of mostly galvanized iron sheeting for roofs and
plank or galvanized sheeting for walls. There seems to
be some feeling of superiority among the inhabitants
of the lower part of the watta against those who live
furthest away from Aluth Mawatha Road. The general
feeling is that those who live higher are indecent,

40

lawless, inclined to violence and not fit to associate with. The temporary shelters made of plank and iron sheeting did not exist in the early stages of the growth of the community.

The neighborhood was earlier known as "Seettu Petti Watta". This name originated from the activities of one Hendrik Perera, the original inhabitant of the storied building at the entrance to the community, who used to own the major part of the location towards Aluth Mawatha Road. Hendrik Perera was a building contractor, who bought all the land right up to public toilets. Earlier he had been living in nearby St. James' Street. He purchased this land from one Fredrik Hudt who returned to his native village of Arabewewa after the sale.

Hendrik Perera, a wealthy man of the area at the time, was held in great respect by the local residents who addressed him by the honorific title "Hendrik Appu". He used to lend money to those in need, taking their jewelry and other valuables as security. He was also the organizer of an informal credit and savings arrangement known as "seettu". Thus this neighborhood began to be known as Seettu Petti Watta. This literally means "lotteries garden" but in this context it means "Pawn Broker's Garden". Hendrik Appu donated land for the construction of the lane that later came to be known as St. Jude's Mawatha, which was only a footpath in his day. According to his descendants, he would loan money even on poor security. It is said that the poor people living near the beach (see Map 3) would in times of need, even leave the family water pot as collateral!

Hendrik Perera married thrice and had a total of ten children. His children were given land and houses from Seettu Petti Watta. During his last years he sold some land, mainly on the left side of the lane where housing units 1, 35, 37, 40 and 43 are situated at

41

present (see Map 4). At the start he lived in a house
near the first water tap on St. Jude's Mawatha. Later
he built a storied house at the entrance to Seettu
Petti Watta and moved there with some of his children.
One of his grand daughters now lives in this storied
building. Other daughters were given rows of houses,
No. 13-15 and 17-20. No. 36 was given to another
daughter who married a Tamil man and is now occupied
by Hendrik Perera's grandson, Joseph Pulle. Some of
Hendrik Appu's descendants sold their land but most
retained ownership, either occupying houses themselves
or renting them. The ownership of houses has now
become fragmented so much so that the storied house
now has five joint owners, none of whom are willing to
undertake the necessary maintenance work in the
building.

The Muthuwella Mawatha end of Jude Mawatha was, in
Hendrik Appu's time (50 years ago), owned by one
Samarasinghe Veda Mahattaya who was also known as
"Hinna Veda" (Hinna caste medical practitioner). At
that time, the Pansal Watta end of Jude Mawatha used
to be called "Hinnagoda Watta" since low-caste Hinna
fisherfolk used to live there. Samarasinghe
Vedamahattaya migrated to the city from Balapitiya and
started a boutique to sell lime for building purposes.
He married a local woman and became wealthy. He also
started treating people for minor ailments and thus
gained the title "Vedamahattaya" (native doctor)
though the abbreviated "Hinna Veda" denotes his low
caste origin. His wealth too, gradually declined in
subsequent years possibly due to illness. In his last
years he sold most of his land.

A name for the lane leading to Seettu Petti Watta
was proposed 20 years ago by V.A. Sugathadasa, the
local M.P. who wished to call it St. Anthony's
Mawatha. However, this was not implemented since there
was already another road called St. Anthony's Mawatha
in Kochchikade. In 1965 Justin Dias who contested the

Municipal Election for this ward, made a vow to St.
Jude's Church, Indigolla promising to honor the saint
if he won. As he won the election, he officially named
the lane leading to Seettu Petti Watta as St. Jude's
Mawatha. Thereafter, the neighborhood too became known
as Jude Mawatha Watta. However, some of the older
inhabitants in the area yet refer to it as Seettu
Petti Watta.

Thus as a low-income neighborhood, Jude mawatha is
at least 50 years old. It is situated in close
proximity to the sea, Colombo harbor and nearby
warehouses (see Map 3). The city center, including
Fort and Pettah areas, is situated within easy reach
of the community. On the whole, it may be described as
an inner-city slum.

TABLE 2.1

THE POPULATION OF JUDE MAWATHA BY SEX AND AGE, 1984

Age Group	Male		Female		Total	
	No.	%	No.	%	No.	%
0 - 5	15	9.5	9	6.3	24	8.0
6 - 14	37	23.4	25	17.4	62	20.5
15 - 24	43	27.2	41	28.5	84	27.8
25 - 44	39	24.7	47	32.6	86	28.5
45 - 60	19	12.0	11	7.6	30	9.9
< 60	5	3.2	11	7.6	16	5.3
Total	158	100.0	144	100.0	302	100.0
Average	24.8		27.9		26.3	

43

In 1984 the community had a total population of 302 distributed in 49 households [1]. The age and sex distribution in the community is given in Table 2.1.

Thus in Jude Mawatha men outnumber women. As regards the age distribution, 28.5 percent of the population is less than 15 years old. Those older than 60 years comprise 5.3 percent of the total population. The average age for the community is 26.3.

SWARNA MAWATHA

The Swarna Mawatha shanty community is situated close to the southern fringe of Colombo. It comes under the CMC Ward of Wellawatta North and electorate of Colombo West (see Map 2). As in the case of Jude Mawatha, this community too is named after the main access road leading to the community. The community is situated on the bank of the Wellawatta Canal directly behind a group of middle-class houses and shops and in close proximity to the Wellawatta Textile Mills (see Map 5). The Swarna Mawatha lane leads away from the High Level Road up to a bridge which crosses the highly polluted Wellawatta canal. The road is tarred up to the bridge. The community under study stretches from Swarna Mawatha on the South to another lane going along the canal bank on the North.

The occupants of Swarna Mawatha maintain conflicting views regarding the origin and subsequent growth of the community, and there are conflicting claims as to who were the earliest to settle down here. An old women whom everyone in the community addresses as "Achchi" (grandmother), claims that only S.D. Somapala was living there when she came in 1949. Somapala helped her to build a cadjan hut, where her entire family lived until 1963 when her daughter built herself a separate hut in a nearby location. Now Achchi's children, grandchildren and great-grandchildren live in separate shanties along the

44

canal bank. Later on, other families obtained permission from her to build on adjoining land, on which Achchi used to cultivate leafy vegetables for home consumption and sale. She was paid an initial sum ranging from Rs.300 to 500 for permitting the use of a housing lot and thereupon a monthly rent of Rs.20 for a shanty unit built by the occupants themselves using their resources. Recently the rent was increased to Rs.30.

Joseph, who at 72 claims to be the oldest inhabitant of the community, says that he came there some time before Achchi. When he came, there were two or three families already living there. He says that most of the original inhabitants subsequently left the community and moved elsewhere.

Many of the older settlers speak of having had to clear the thick under-growth in order to build their shanties. The newcomers had to pay the original inhabitants for the right to build on these lands. Most persons came here because they had been asked to vacate their former houses and they were told by friends or relatives about availability of vacant land in Swarna Mawatha. By the late 1970s most of the land available had been occupied.

The identity of the rightful owner of the land in Swarna Mawatha is obscure. Some local residents are of the opinion that the land belongs to the Land Reclamation Board as was stated by a visiting policeman. However, other shanty dwellers believe that a stretch of 20 feet on either bank of the canal belongs to the Irrigation Department since they had been told so by some engineers who had come to clear the canal several years ago. The same engineers are reported to have said that the rest of the land in Swarna Mawatha belongs to the CMC.

45

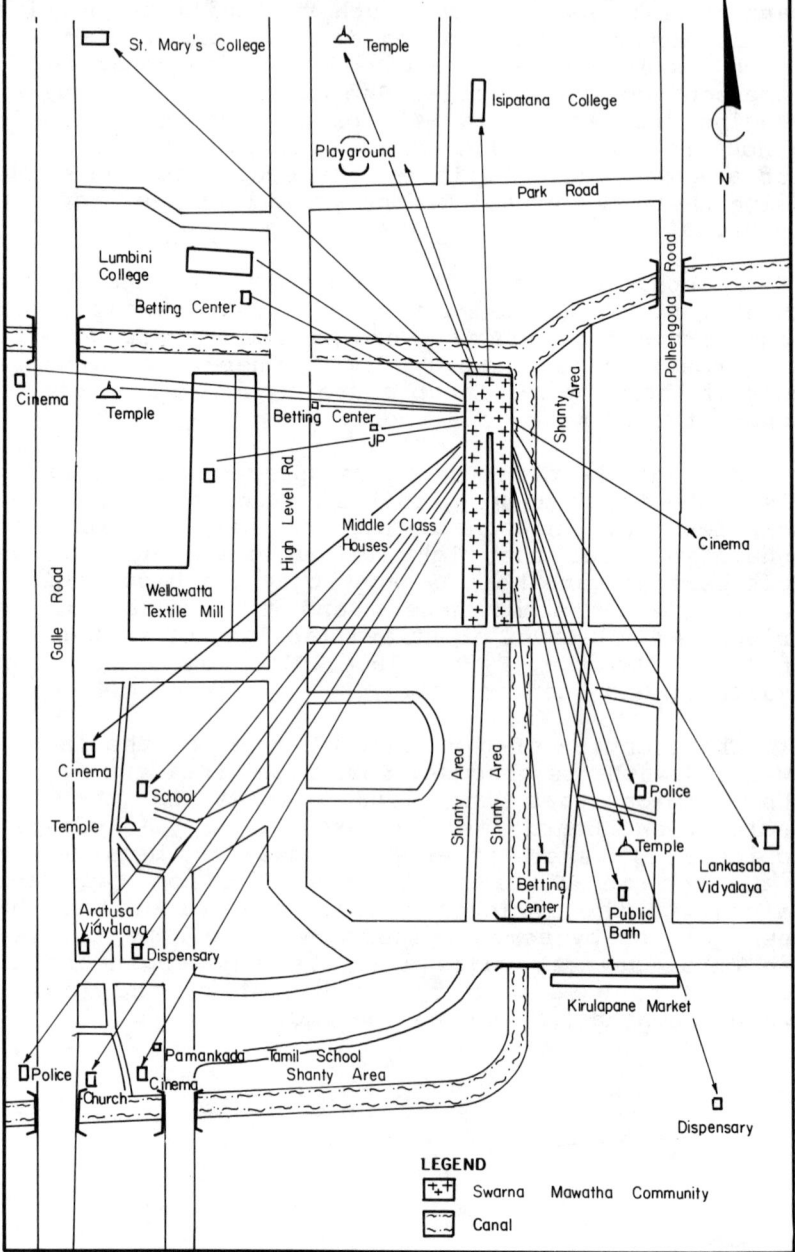

Map 5 : **MAP SHOWING THE SURROUNDINGS OF SWARNA MAWATHA**

St. Mary's College

Temple

Isipatana College

Playground

Park Road

Polhengoda Road

Lumbini College

Betting Center

Cinema

Temple

Betting Center
JP

High Level Rd

Middle Class Houses

Wellawatta Textile Mill

Galle Road

Shanty Area

Cinema

Cinema

Temple

School

Police

Temple

Aratusa Vidyalaya

Shanty Area

Shanty Area

Betting Center

Lankasaba Vidyalaya

Dispensary

Public Bath

Kirulapane Market

Police

Church

Cinema

Pamankada Tamil School
Shanty Area

Dispensary

LEGEND

Swarna Mawatha Community

Canal

N

Map 6 : SWARNA MAWATHA COMMUNITY MAP

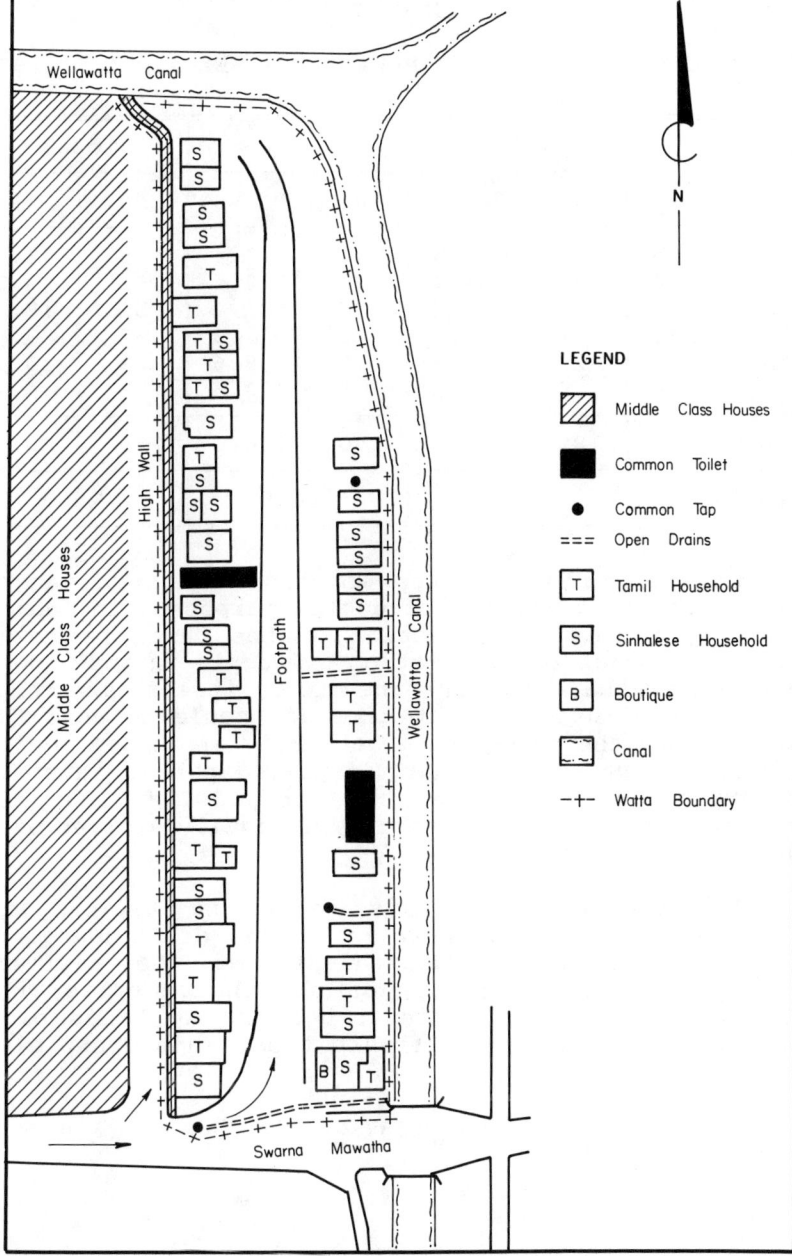

Wellawatta Canal

Middle Class Houses

High Wall

Footpath

Wellawatta Canal

Swarna Mawatha

N

LEGEND

Middle Class Houses

Common Toilet

Common Tap

=== Open Drains

T Tamil Household

S Sinhalese Household

B Boutique

Canal

—+— Watta Boundary

TABLE   2.2

THE POPULATION OF SWARNA MAWATHA BY SEX AND AGE, 1984

Age Group	Male		Female		Total	
	No.	%	No.	%	No.	%
0 - 5	20	14.8	16	11.4	36	13.1
6 - 14	33	24.4	31	22.1	64	23.3
15 - 24	21	15.6	30	21.4	51	18.6
25 - 44	36	26.7	46	32.9	82	29.8
45 - 60	17	12.6	12	8.6	29	10.5
< 60	8	5.9	5	3.6	13	4.7
Total	135	100.0	140	100.0	275	100.
Average	25.7		24.9		25.3	

In the early days the location had much vacant land used for a variety of public purposes, including grazing of cattle. A section of the canal bank was used as a place for defecation by people in and around Swarna Mawatha. However, the canal itself was relatively unpolluted at that time and could be used for bathing. As the number of inhabitants in the community rapidly increased, the CMC installed public latrines in Swarna Mawatha during the early 1970s. Thus the Swarna Mawatha shanty community gradually evolved over the past 40 years.

All the dwelling units in Swarna Mawatha are shanties (see Map 6). There is a total of 51 houses in this community. The descendants of the earliest settlers "own" a majority of the shanty units; the shanty ownership is concentrated in the hands of a certain group bound by kinship ties. This group also

48

controls leadership in the community as will be elaborated later.

The Swarna Mawatha community consists of two parallel rows of shanties situated on either side of a footpath (see Map 6). The shanties on the canal bank side have more space, including some space for gardening. Some of the shanties on the opposite side of the footpath are built against a high wall separating neighboring middle-class houses from Swarna Mawatha; these shanty units are made of cadjan, galvanized sheets or a combination of both. Most of the units on the canal bank side have mud walls, cadjan roofs, and cement floors. The inhabitants get drinking water from common taps and use common toilets.

In 1984 there was a total of 275 people in the community distributed in 51 households. According to Table 2.2, in Swarna Mawatha, unlike in the other three communities studied, males are outnumbered by females. The under 15 age group comprises 26.4 percent of the total population. Those over 60 years of age comprise nearly five percent of the population. The average age for the community is 25.3.

SOYZA LANE

This was a central city slum situated in the heart of Kandy. Fieldwork in this community was carried out in 1984. Subsequently (in 1986) the community was relocated by the Kandy Municipal Council (KMC) in a new site on the southern fringe of the city. The description given here relates to the conditions in this inner-city slum prior to the relocation of its inhabitants.

At the time of the study (1984) the Soyza Lane slum community had a total population of 195 distributed in 33 households. In addition, the community had an unknown number of temporary residents who used

49

Map 7 : **MAP SHOWING THE SURROUNDINGS OF SOYZA LANE**

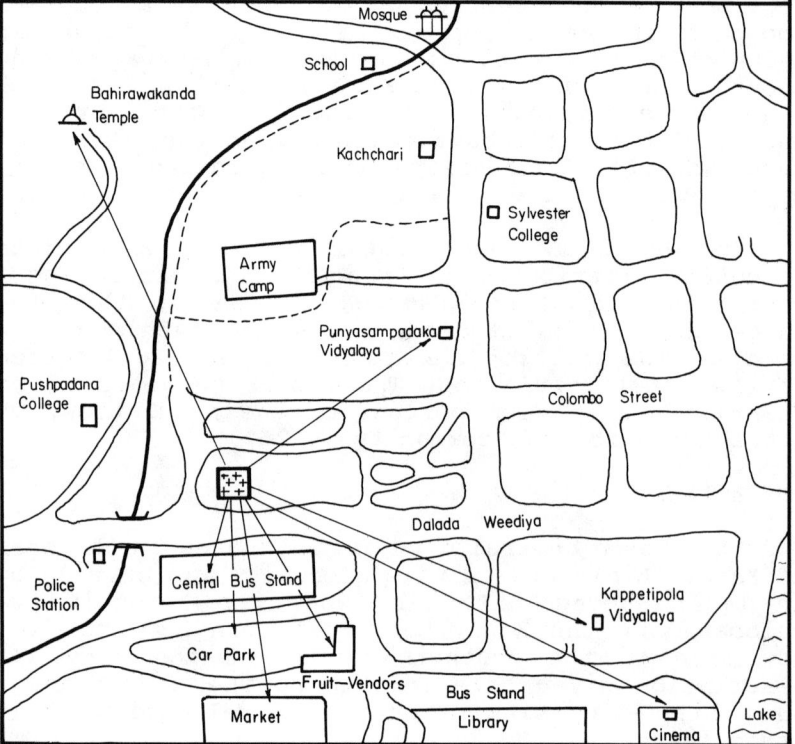

N

Mosque

School

Bahirawakanda
Temple

Kachchari

Sylvester
College

Army
Camp

Punyasampadaka
Vidyalaya

Pushpadana
College

Colombo   Street

Dalada   Weediya

Police
Station

Central Bus Stand

Kappetipola
Vidyalaya

Car Park

Fruit—Vendors

Bus Stand

Market

Library

Cinema

Lake

LEGEND

Soyza Lane Community

Street

Railway   Line

Footpath

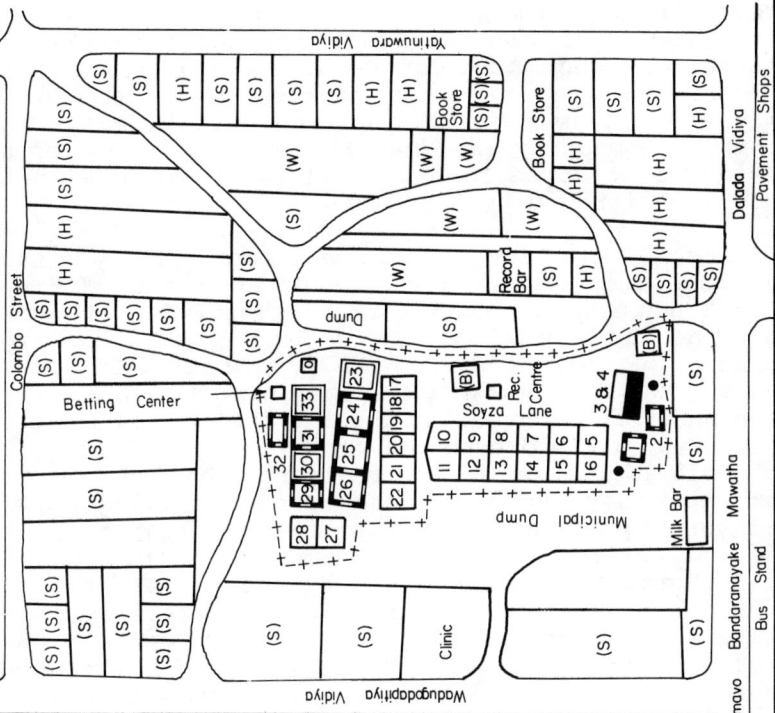

Map 8 : SOYZA LANE COMMUNITY MAP

LEGEND

	Labor Line
	Shanty Unit
	New Cement House
	Common Toilet
–+–	Watta Boundary
(W)	Warehouse
(B)	Boutique
(H)	Hotel / Cafe
(S)	Shop
•	Common Tap
——	Railway Line

N

Yatinuwara Vidiya

Dalada Vidiya

Pavement Shops

Book Store

Record Bar

Colombo Street

Betting Center

Soyza Lane

Rec. Centre

3 8 4

Municipal Dump

Dump

Milk Bar

Mawatha

Bandaranayake

Bus Stand

Sirimavo

Wadugodapitiya Vidiya

Clinic

Railway Line

Bahirawakanda Temple

Pushpadana College

Soyza Lane as a base for several illegal operations. A greater part of the neighborhood consisted of several rows of attached houses built over sixty years ago as labor quarters for road workers under the Public Works Department (PWD). Since the community was located in a back alley covered by several commercial establishments facing the main road, it was well suited for various illegal operations (see Map 8). Access to the community was through the narrow Soyza Lane from which the community got its name [2]. The Central Bus Stand, the Central Market, both authorized and unauthorized pavement hawking areas within the city and the railway station were within easy reach from the community (see Map 7). The livelihood of the residents of Soyza Lane were closely linked with the above-mentioned city locations.

According to the oldest inhabitants of Soyza Lane, the community began in the 1920s as a set of "labor lines" housing the road workers employed by the PWD. Most of the original residents, i.e., the road workers, had migrated from the low country. During the 1940s, due to unknown circumstances the labor lines came under the control of the KMC from the PWD. At the same time, again due to the unknown circumstances, the economic activities of the residents changed from road work to other types of urban work including hawking and working as porters in the markets (natami work). The character and even the composition of the community gradually changed and by the 1950s, it became a prime center for various illegal operations in the city, including prostitution, gambling, picking pockets and sale of illicit liquor. Partly in response to these developments and partly in consideration of the potential commercial value of this central city location, the KMC became interested in relocating the inhabitants of Soyza Lane since the late 1950s. This led to a bitter confrontation between the community and the KMC. The struggle between the KMC and the community continued in the 1960s and 1970s with

52

neither party being able to achieve a victory. Finally, at the end of a long battle, the inhabitants of Soyza Lane were shifted to a new site at the edge of the city in April 1986.

TABLE 2.3

THE POPULATION OF SOYZA LANE BY SEX AND AGE, 1984

Age Group	Male		Female		Total	
	No.	%	No.	%	No.	%
0 - 5	17	16.3	13	14.2	30	15.4
6 - 14	26	25.0	33	36.3	59	30.2
15 - 24	28	26.9	13	14.3	41	21.0
25 - 44	26	25.0	22	24.2	48	24.6
45 - 60	5	4.8	9	9.9	14	7.2
< 60	2	2.0	1	1.0	3	1.6
Total	104	100.0	91	100.0	195	100.0
Average	21.6		21.0		20.8	

In this community males outnumbered females in a ratio of 1 to 1.1 (see Table 2.3). A total of 45.6 percent of the population were below 15 years of age. The elderly, i.e., those older than 60 years, constituted 1.6 percent of the population. The average age of its population was 20.8. On the whole this community had a younger population when compared to the other three communities.

KAMACHCHODE

Kamachchode is one of several low-income neighborhoods in the coastal city of Negombo which had a total population of 60,762 in 1981. Situated on the

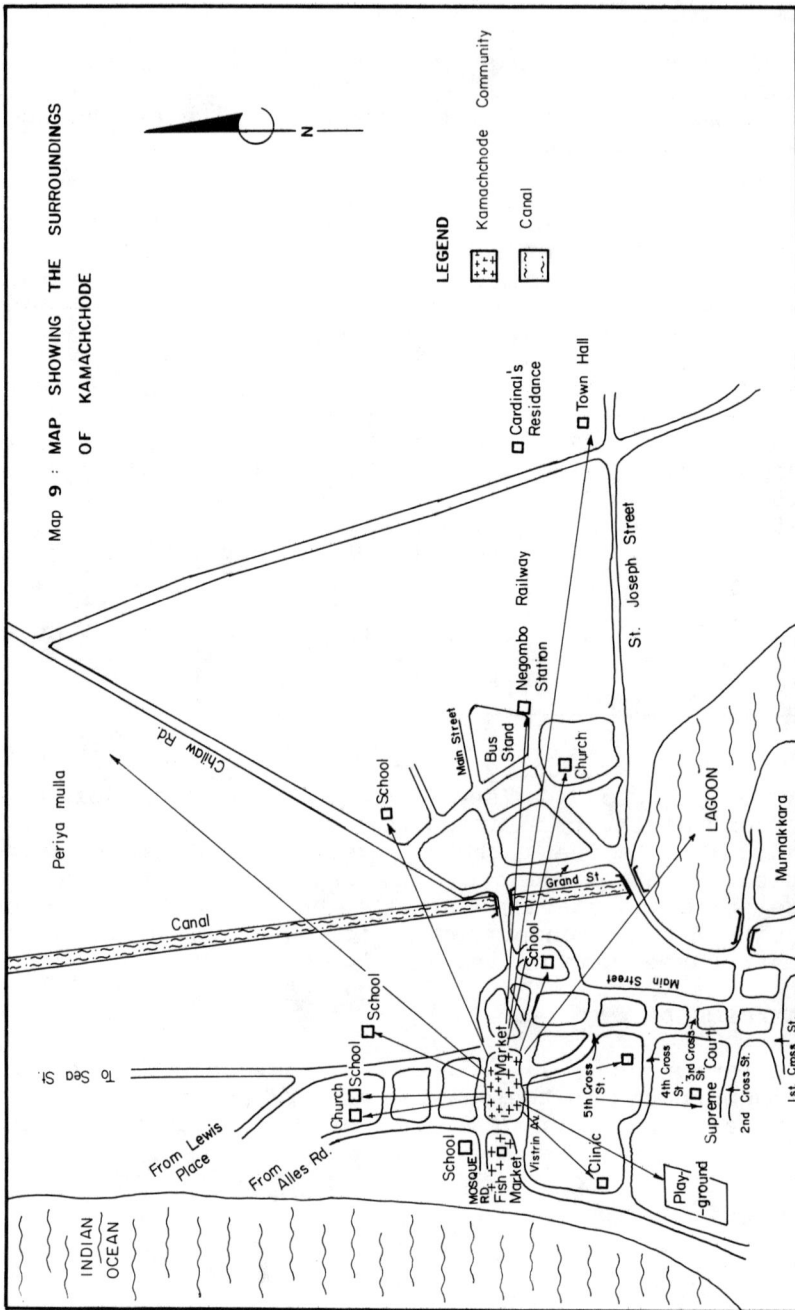

Map 9 : MAP SHOWING THE SURROUNDINGS OF KAMACHCHODE

LEGEND

Kamachchode Community

Canal

N

Periya mulla

Chilaw Rd.

Canal

INDIAN OCEAN

To Sea St.

From Lewis Place

From Alles Rd.

School

Church

School

School

MOSQUE

RD.

Fish Market

Vistrin Av.

Market

Clinic

Play-ground

School

5th Cross St.

4th Cross St.

3rd Cross St.

Supreme Court

2nd Cross St.

1st Cross St.

Main Street

School

Grand St.

Main Street

Bus Stand

Negombo Railway Station

Church

St. Joseph Street

Cardinal's Residance

Town Hall

LAGOON

Munnakkara

Map 10 : KAMACHCHODE COMMUNITY MAP

LEGEND

41	Household Number
□	Municipal House
▣	Shanty
☐	New Cement House
▨	Middle Class Houses
■	Common Toilet
●	Common Tap
—+—	Watta Boundary
(S)	Store

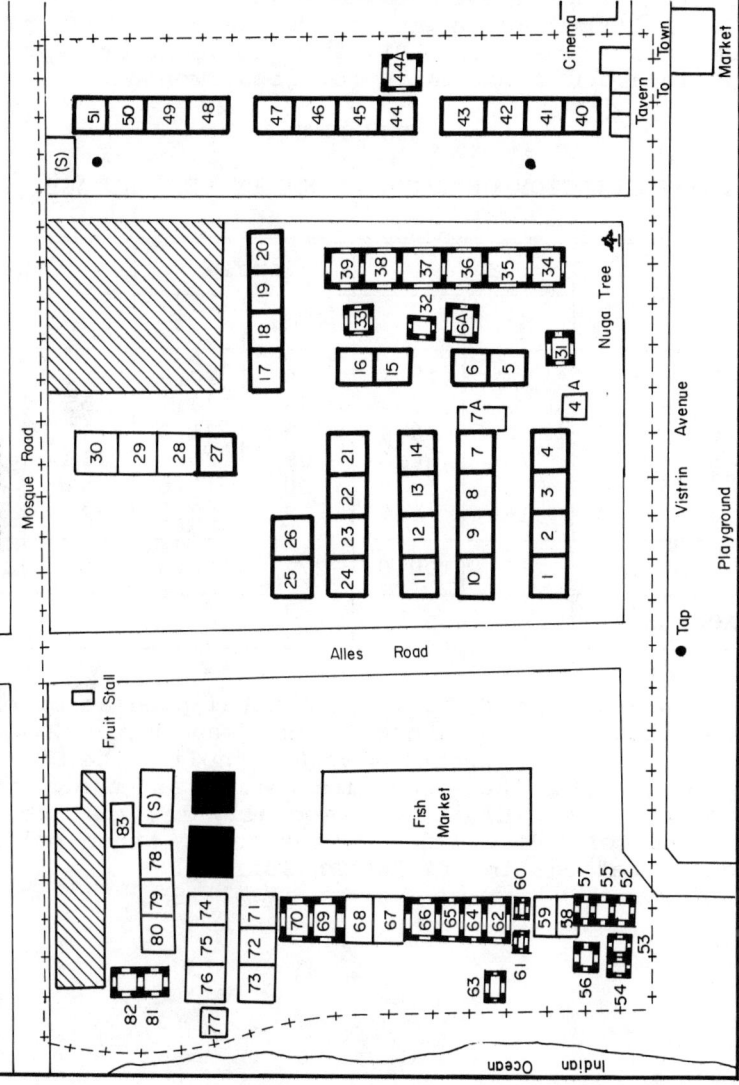

N

Mosque

Muslim School

Mosque Road

Alles Road

Fruit Stall

Fish Market

Nuga Tree

Vistrin Avenue

Playground

● Tap

Cinema

Tavern

To Town

Market

Indian Ocean

beach, Kamachchode is only ten minutes away on foot
from the busy streets of Negombo. It consists mainly
of a row of shanties stretching along the beach and a
neighboring housing project built for local fishermen
in 1956. The principal occupation of both the shanty
dwellers and the inhabitants of the housing scheme is
fishing. The Old Fish Market situated in the middle of
the neighborhood also serves as a center of the
community (see Map 10). The Fish Market provides
income avenues specially for local women.

TABLE 2.4

THE POPULATION OF KAMACHCHODE BY SEX AND AGE, 1984

Age Group	Male		Female		Total	
	No.	%	No.	%	No.	%
0 - 5	34	12.1	28	10.3	62	11.2
6 - 14	77	27.3	78	28.7	155	28.0
15 - 24	52	18.4	58	21.3	110	19.8
25 - 44	70	24.8	69	25.4	139	25.1
45 - 60	33	11.8	30	11.0	63	11.4
< 60	16	5.7	9	3.3	25	4.5
Total	282	100.0	272	100.0	554	100.0
Average	25.2		24.0		24.6	

In 1984 Kamachchode had a total population of 554
distributed in 83 households (see Table 2.4); 75
percent of the households were Catholic. The Sinhalese
Catholics in the area use Tamil as their mother
tongue, thus exhibiting a socially marginal position
in relation to the mainstream ethno-religious
concentrations in Sri Lankan Society.

Of the two segments in the neighborhood, the shanty component is much older than the housing scheme. The shanty dwellers consider themselves the original inhabitants of the area. They have myths that connect them to the patron saint for the sea, St. Sebastian. The housing scheme built in 1956 was made available to selected low-income families from Kamachchode and several neighboring communities. Between 1956 and 1984 many of the housing units put up under the scheme had rapidly deteriorated, giving rise to a slum-like atmosphere in this section of the neighborhood.

In Kamachchode the number of males slightly exceeds that of females (see Table 2.4). Those under 15 years of age constitute 39.2 percent of the population. The elderly (i.e. those older than 60 years) comprise 4.5 percent of the total population. The average age for the community is 24.6.

SOME COMPARISONS

In this section we further examine the characteristics of the four communities studied by comparing them in respect to certain selected variables.

Table 2.5 summarizes information about the size of the communities.

Thus according to the population size, the largest community is Kamachchode, followed by Jude Mawatha, Swarna Mawatha and Soyza Lane. The average numbers of households and inhabitants per study community are 54 and 330 respectively as compared with 35 households and 220 inhabitants per community discovered by Tilakaratna et al. (1984). The average number of persons per household for all four communities is 6.1; it varies from 5.4 in Swarna Mawatha to 6.7 in Kamachchode.

TABLE 2.5

SIZE OF COMMUNITIES

Community	Total No. of Households	Total Population	Ave. No. of Persons per Household
Jude Mawatha	49	302	6.2
Swarna Mawatha	51	275	5.4
Soyza Lane	33	195	5.9
Kamachchode	83	554	6.7
Total	216	1,326	6.1
Average	54	331.5	-

Data concerning the length of stay in the community are given in Table 2.6.

Clearly, the watta population is not a transient one as is assumed by certain authors. The communities studied consists of long-established stable populations, with household heads continuously living in the same communities for an average of 20 years. About 75 percent of the household heads have been continuously living in their present neighborhoods for ten years or more. In terms of the reported length of stay of household heads, the most stable community is Soyza Lane followed by Jude Mawatha, Kamachchode and Swarna Mawatha. However, it is possible that those in Soyza Lane exaggerated their length of stay in the community in view of their campaign against the relocation efforts of the CMC. On the whole the data point to the longer history of slum communities (Soyza Lane and Jude Mawatha) as against shanty communities.

TABLE 2.6

HOW LONG THE HEAD OF THE HOUSEHOLD HAS BEEN LIVING IN THE PRESENT COMMUNITY

Period (Years)	Jude Mawatha		Swarna Mawatha		Soyza Lane		Kamachchode		All	
	f	%	f	%	f	%	f	%	f	%
> 1	7	14.3	2	3.9	0	0	1	1.2	10	4.6
1 - 5	2	4.1	9	17.7	0	0	9	10.9	20	9.2
5 - 10	0	0	13	25.5	4	12.1	8	9.6	25	11.6
10 - 20	12	24.5	15	29.4	4	12.1	18	21.7	49	22.7
< 20	28	57.1	12	23.5	25	75.8	47	56.6	112	51.9
Total	49	100.0	51	100.0	33	100.0	83	100.0	216	100.0
Average	21.1		15.6		24.5		20.2		20.1	
Standard Deviation	11.4		12.2		9.4		11.2		11.0	

TABLE 2.7

DISTRIBUTION OF HOUSEHOLDS BY PLACE OF BIRTH OF HEAD OF HOUSEHOLD

Place of Birth	Jude Mawatha		Swarna Mawatha		Soyza Lane		Kamachchode		All	
	f	%	f	%	f	%	f	%	f	%
Present watta	10	20.4	2	3.9	18	54.5	15	18.1	45	20.8
Other watta in the same town	17	34.8	13	25.5	5	15.2	46	55.4	81	37.5
Other place in the same town	1	2.0	4	7.8	0	0	3	3.6	8	3.7
Other town	8	16.3	9	17.6	8	24.2	13	15.7	38	17.6
Village	12	24.5	7	13.7	2	6.1	2	2.4	23	10.6
Estate	1	2.0	11	21.6	0	0	0	0	12	5.6
No information	0	0		9.9	0	0	4	4.8	9	4.2
Total	49	100.0	51	100.0	33	100.0	83	100.0	216	100.0

Table 2.7 shows that nearly 21 percent of households in the four communities are headed by people born within the same communities. Of those who had moved from outside, a substantial number, i.e. 37.5 percent of all households, had moved from other watta communities in the same town. It follows that the inflow of excess population from the older watta communities in the same town was a major factor that led to the growth of new watta communities. Another significant findings is that a total of 62 percent of the households are headed by those native to the respective towns. The heads of another 17.5 percent of the households have migrated from other, possibly smaller, towns. Thus nearly 80 percent of all household heads in the four locations are of urban origin. Only 16.2 percent of the watta household heads originally came from rural areas covering villages and estates. Of the four communities studied, Jude Mawatha received a considerable influx from the villages, Soyza Lane from other towns and Swarna Mawatha from the estates. It must be stressed, however, that none of the communities has received an exceedingly large influx of rural people.

HOUSING CONDITIONS

Some preliminary data regarding housing conditions in the four communities are presented in Tables 2.8 to 2.10.

According to Table 2.8, the predominant house type in the communities studied is shanties followed by old houses, the Municipal Housing, new permanent structures and labor lines. The predominant house type in Jude Mawatha is old houses, in Swarna Mawatha shanties, in Soyza Lane labor lines and in Kamachchode Municipal Houses. Shanties, old houses and some newly-built permanent houses exist in all four communities studied.

TABLE 2.8

DISTRIBUTION OF HOUSEHOLDS ACCORDING TO TYPE OF DWELLING UNIT

Type of Dwelling	Jude Mawatha		Swarna Mawatha		Soyza Lane		Kamachchode		All	
	f	%	f	%	f	%	f	%	f	%
Shanties	10	20.4	45	88.2	8	24.2	29	35.0	92	42.6
Labor Lines	0	0	0	0	14	42.5	0	0	14	6.5
Old Houses	36	73.5	3	5.9	8	24.2	8	9.6	55	25.5
Municipal Housing	0	0	0	0	0	0	39	47.0	39	18.0
Permanent Buildings	3	6.1	3	5.9	3	9.1	7	8.4	16	7.4
Total	49	100.0	51	100.0	33	100.0	83	100.0	216	100.0

TABLE 2.9

DISTRIBUTION OF HOUSEHOLDS ACCORDING TO PATTERN OF CLUSTERING

Pattern of Clustering	Jude Mawatha		Swarna Mawatha		Soyza Lane		Kamach- chode		Total	
	f	%	f	%	f	%	f	%	f	%
Attached Houses	41	83.7	21	41.2	30	90.9	71	85.5	163	75.5
Row Houses	0	0	16	31.4	0	0	0	0	16	7.4
Detached Houses	8	16.3	14	27.4	3	9.1	12	14.5	37	17.1
Total	49	100.0	51	100.0	33	100.0	83	100.0	216	100.0

TABLE 2.10

DISTRIBUTION OF HOUSEHOLDS ACCORDING TO TENURIAL STATUS

Tenurial Status	Jude Mawatha		Swarna Mawatha		Soyza Lane		Kamach- chode		All	
	f	%	f	%	f	%	f	%	f	%
Owner-Occupant	21	42.9	0	0	0	0	47	56.6	68	31.5
Tenant	20	40.8	24	47.1	0	0	12	14.5	56	25.9
Lessee	2	4.1	0	0	0	0	1	1.2	3	1.4
Rent-free Tenant	6	12.2	0	0	0	0	11	13.2	17	7.9
Squatter	0	0	25	49.0	33	100.0	12	14.5	70	32.4
Other	0	0	2	3.9	0	0	0	0	2	0.9
Total	49	100.0	51	100.0	33	100.0	83	100.0	216	100.0

Table 2.9 shows that in the case of 75.5 percent of the households, the housing units are physically attached to other housing units. A further 7.4 percent of the households are compactly arranged in the form of rows of houses. Only 17.1 percent of the households exist as fully detached units. Swarna Mawatha and Jude Mawatha have the highest proportion of attached dwelling units.

In terms of tenurial status (see Table 2.10) a majority of the households are squatters followed closely by owner-occupants; 27 percent of the households are rent-paying tenants. The highest proportion of owner-occupancy is in Kamachchode followed by Jude Mawatha. Squatting is most common in Soyza Lane followed by Swarna Mawatha.

In summary, the watta communities under study are quite small in size, over 30 years old as low-income neighborhoods and have relatively stable populations. For the most part they are hidden away in back alleys and other such "backyards" of the city, in ways that conceal their magnitude or even presence from the casual visitors to the towns. Many of the watta household heads are of urban origin, indicating that natural growth within the cities rather than rural-urban migration per se has been the main factor affecting the growth of watta communities over the past few decades. There is considerable variation among the watta communities in respect to their size, composition, housing and neighborhood characteristics, accessibility and various other attributes.

NOTES

1. In this study a household is defined as a housing unit within which food is shared on a daily basis. The practice of common cooking is not reckoned as a definitive feature of a household in view of the fact

that home cooking is relatively insignificant in one of the study communities.

2. However, the community was more widely known by its rather disreputable name "Alimudukkuwa" (lit. Elephant Slum, but it also means "Huge Slum"). This name is believed to have derived from the fact that an elephant running away from the Kandy Perahara was finally shot down near this neighborhood.

CHAPTER THREE

WATTA ECONOMY

Recent studies indicate that the informal sector constitutes an important segment of the urban economy of Sri Lanka. A study conducted by the Marga Institute in 1978 estimated that 19.3 percent of the total work force in Colombo was employed in the informal sector (Marga Institute 1979a: 27). Further, it was found that the informal sector has a high labor absorption capacity and that the cost-effectiveness of the services rendered by it to the larger city population is quite high.

As the Marga study referred to above was based on a citywide sample of informal sector economic units, it could not fully uncover the community dimensions of the informal sector economy in urban Sri Lanka. The following statements, however, indicate that a community approach is necessary for fully understanding the informal sector activities.

> The localities in which the tenement type housing predominates are those in which the low-income economic activities and participation in the informal sector is high (p.13).

> The informal sector activities are therefore not merely economic activities that can be investigated and analyzed as such. They are an inseparable part of the whole socio-economic complex with its own ways of

living, its own social norms and its codes
of conduct regarding recruitment and operation (p.114-115).

The present chapter describes the economic
activities of the four communities studied, focusing
on their connections with the informal sector in each
city. Following the Marga study (1979a:25), the
present study defines a certain economic unit as an
informal sector unit if it shows the following combination of features.

1. employs less than five persons at a time.
2. maintained as a family enterprise.
3. capital investment and level of technology are
   low.
4. bookkeeping and other formal managerial
   devices are kept to a minimum.
5. the required skills have been obtained mostly
   outside the formal education system.

Using the above definition, the overall significance
of the informal sector in the economic activities of
the four communities studied will be assessed.

EMPLOYMENT PATTERN

Table 3.1 presents the sectoral distribution of
the workers in the study population (i.e. combined
population in all four communities) by sex and occupational categories. In the household survey the respondents were asked to describe the primary and secondary
occupations of each household member currently earning
an income. Table 3.1 gives the distribution of workers
according to their primary occupations determined on
the basis of income. A detailed breakdown of occupational categories is given so as to illustrate the
full complexity of the employment situation in the
watta communities.

Thus out of a total population of 1,318, 422 or 32 percent are reportedly engaged in economic activities of some kind. In regard to the overall distribution of workers according to employment categories, the following points emerge from Table 3.1. First, manual labor is the single most important means of livelihood in the study population. Nearly 32 percent of the economically active are engaged in laboring jobs of some kind as their primary occupation. This shows the predominantly working-class character of the four communities studied. Further 13 percent of the workers are itinerant day laborers, meaning that they have no assured means of livelihood and must struggle daily to secure income-earning opportunities. A good example of a worker in this category is the load carrier, referred to as "natami" in the watta parlance; they offer their services to potential clients in a competitive manner, usually on busy streets with their "carrying hooks" in their hands.

As for the other laboring categories the casual laborers are usually employed on a full-time basis in a firm of some kind, but they are not granted full employee status and the accompanying benefits, like salary increments, paid leave and promotions; further, the firms reserve the right to retrench these workers at short notice when necessary. The sanitary laborers, who are few in number, normally have guaranteed employment, but socially they are treated as outcasts. Finally, the skilled workers comprising nine percent of the economically active, range from carpenters to printing workers. They are distinguished from the other laboring categories by virtue of the fact that they have gone through a period of apprenticeship. Normally their wages are considerably higher than those of the other laboring categories. They may also possess a few tools of their own. Employment opportunities, however, can be quite irregular for some of the skilled categories.

TABLE 3.1

SECTORAL DISTRIBUTION OF WORKERS IN ALL FOUR COMMUNITIES
BY SEX AND OCCUPATIONAL CATEGORY
(percentages)

Employment	Formal Sector			Informal Sector			Grand Total
	Male	Female	Total	Male	Female	Total	
Labor (Total)	66.7	14.3	61.4	32.0	14.2	25.8	31.7
Itinerant Day Laborer	0	0	0	17.8	11.7	15.6	13.0
Casual Laborer	47.6	0	42.8	3.0	0	2.0	8.8
Sanitary Laborer	1.6	14.3	2.9	0	1.7	0.6	0.9
Skilled Worker	17.5	0	15.7	11.2	0.8	7.6	9.0
Trade (Total)	3.2	28.6	5.7	33.3	22.5	29.6	25.6
Boutique/Shop Asst.	1.6	0	1.4	5.2	0	3.4	3.1
Pavement Hawker-Mobile	0	0	0	11.2	15.0	12.5	10.4
Pavement Hawker-Fixed	0	0	0	2.2	0	1.4	1.2
Boutique Keeper	0	0	0	2.2	0	1.4	1.2
Market Trader	0	0	0	0.9	0	0.6	0.5
Illicit Selling	0	0	0	2.6	6.7	4.0	3.3
Other	1.6	28.6	4.3	9.0	0.8	6.3	5.9
Domestic Servants (Total)	0	0	0	2.6	47.5	18.2	15.2
Employed Locally	0	0	0	0	15.0	5.4	4.5
Employed Abroad	0	0	0	2.6	32.5	12.8	10.7

TABLE 3.1 Continued.

Employment	Formal Sector			Informal Sector			Grand Total
	Male	Female	Total	Male	Female	Total	
Services (Total)	30.1	57.1	32.8	16.9	9.9	14.4	17.4
Clerk/Technician	4.8	0	4.3	0	0	0	0.7
Forces/Security Guard	4.8	0	4.3	0	0	0	0.7
Driver	1.6	0	1.4	5.7	0	3.6	3.3
Tailor/Machinist	1.6	57.1	7.2	1.3	5.8	2.8	3.6
Cook	1.6	0	1.4	4.3	0.8	3.2	2.8
Tourist Guide	1.6	0	1.4	2.6	0.8	2.0	1.9
Waiter/Hotel Servant	0	0	0	1.7	0.8	1.1	0.9
Transport Worker	1.6	0	1.4	0.4	0	0.6	0.7
Other	12.5	0	11.4	0.9	1.7	1.1	2.8
Other (Total)	0	0	0	15.1	5.8	12.1	10.0
Junk Dealer	0	0	0	0.4	0.8	0.6	0.5
Fisherman	0	0	0	12.5	0.8	8.5	7.1
Prostitute	0	0	0	0	1.7	0.6	0.5
Betting	0	0	0	0.9	0	0.6	0.5
Money Lender	0	0	0	1.3	0	0.9	0.7
Miscellaneous	0	0	0	0	2.5	0.9	0.7
GRAND TOTAL	100.0	100.0	100.0	100.0	100.0	100.0	100.0
SAMPLE SIZE	63	7	70	32	120	352	422
TOTAL SECTOR-WISE	70 (16.6%)			352 (83.4%)			

Second, after manual labor the most important economic activity in the study population is petty trade. Nearly 26 percent of the economically active are connected with petty trade.

Of the various trading activities among the watta residents, pavement hawking is the most important; nearly 12 percent of all the economically active are engaged in hawking either as mobile traders or as hawkers with fixed stalls. The hawkers in turn range from women selling fish or fruit in large baskets (watti) to ice cream vendors on bicycles or tricycles. Most of the traders from the watta communities obtain their supplies from higher level traders either on credit or on a profit-sharing basis. Their business often border on illegal operations due to the nature of the merchandise (i.e. illicit liquor), where it is sold (i.e. zones of the city where hawking is prohibited) or how it is sold (i.e. without using licensed weighing instruments etc.). As will be elaborated later, their place of residence is critically important in gaining access to strategically important business venues. One's rise from being a shop assistant or hawker to a market trader indicates an important line of upward mobility, at times leading to migration out of the watta communities.

Finally, the other income-earning activities among the watta residents include fishing, collection of discarded bottles and other reusable material, prostitution, betting and money lending. As will be elaborated, fishing is an important economic activity in Kamachchode, situated on the Negombo beach. Both prostitution and betting are unlawful activities engaged in by a few persons in the respective communities. The actual number involved in these activities, however, may be considerably higher than the number who admitted to be engaged in them.

THE SECTORAL DISTRIBUTION OF WORKERS

Table 3.1 shows that 83.4 percent of the workers from the watta communities are engaged in informal sector activities, as against 16.6 percent of the workers employed in the formal sector. This reveals the overwhelming significance of the informal sector in relation to the watta communities. As noted earlier, the Marga study estimated that as of 1978, 19 percent of the total employed population in Colombo city was engaged in the informal sector. This figure is for all income groups in Colombo city. According to UDA estimates, more than a half of the population in Colombo live in low-income communities of one kind or another. The findings of the present study show that over 80 percent of the economically active in the selected watta communities are actually employed in the informal sector[1]. On this basis we are inclined to think that the actual number of informal sector workers in Colombo city may be much higher than the number estimated by the Marga study. The workers employed in certain categories of informal sector activities, such as illegal operations, appear to have been excluded from the Marga study. The analysis of the employment pattern in the wattas indicate that the livelihood of the watta residents hinges mostly on the informal sector in each city.

As for gender differences in respect of employment, it is evident that compared to males a much higher proportion of female workers are engaged in the informal sector. Some 120 out of a total of 127 female workers (94.5 percent) are employed in the informal sector as against 232 out of 295 male workers (78.6 percent). This implies that with a few exceptions the female workers in the wattas are by and large restricted to certain selected employment categories where the worst employment conditions prevail.

73

Most of the formal sector workers from the watta communities are employed as skilled or unskilled laborers in government or privately-owned warehouses and factories. Some of the watta residents are employed in certain outcast occupations falling within the formal sector, such as sanitary labor. Certain service occupations belonging to the semi-skilled category account for the remaining formal sector employment opportunities accessible to the urban poor. The leading informal sector opportunity in the watta communities studied is petty trade, followed by manual labor, work as domestic servants and other types of service occupations.

As a substantial number of women from the watta communities were employed abroad, i.e. in the Middle East, it received special attention in this study.

MIDDLE-EAST EMPLOYMENT

Employment opportunities in the Middle East have given rise to an enhanced degree of economic dynamism among the urban poor in Sri Lanka since 1979 or so. In 1983 nearly 11 percent of the economically active in the four communities studied were currently employed in the Middle East. Among women 39 out of a total of 127 working women or 30.7 percent were employed in the Middle East mainly as domestic servants. Of the four communities studied, all except Soyza Lane had significant numbers currently working in the Middle East.

The monthly income of a Middle-East worker from the watta communities was in the region of Rs.2,000 to 3,000. Although this was considerably higher than what they could possibly earn from the categories of employment available locally, in terms of other employment conditions, such as method of recruitment, levels of skills required and the general working conditions, the Middle-East employment had much in

74

common with the informal sector opportunities available locally. In some instances those working in the
Middle East had got down some of their family members
to work along-side them, replicating the kinship-based
recruitment pattern prevailing in the informal sector.
Further, as in other informal sector activities, the
immigrant workers in the Middle East were minimally
protected against excesses by the employers.

Details in regard to actual and prospective
Middle-East workers in the four communities are given
in Table 3.2.

TABLE   3.2

STATUS WITH REGARD TO MIDDLE-EAST EMPLOYMENT

Category	JM	SM	SL	KM	All
Number currently working in the Middle East	24	12	1	9	46
Number returned from a period of work in the Middle East	16	3	1	10	30
Number actively seeking Middle-East employment	20	13	12	14	59
Total	60	28	14	33	135
Above as a % of work force	30.0	17.3	14.5	10.6	17.4

JM = Jude Mawatha   SM = Swarna Mawatha
SL = Soyza Lane   KM = Kamachchode

It is evident that in each community, apart from those currently employed in the Middle-East countries, there is a considerable number of people who have returned from employment in the Middle East. Moreover, there are many who are actively seeking to obtain Middle-East employment by way of having the necessary advance money paid, having the required papers ready and so on. According to Table 3.2, the highest participation in Middle-East employment is recorded in Jude Mawatha, followed by Swarna Mawatha, Soyza Lane and Kamachchode. On the whole the tendency to seek foreign employment appears to be much greater in watta communities in Colombo compared to those in provincial towns. However, it is quite significant that 17.4 percent of the total work force in all four communities comprises of actual or prospective Middle-East workers. It can be said that roughly one out of every two households in these communities has been directly affected by Middle-East employment.

All in all, the opening of employment avenues in the Middle East for a category of watta-dwellers has led to considerable social and economic changes in watta communities. As an outcome of this new employment avenue the money supply within these communities has substantially increased, an aspect which is critically important for understanding the emerging trends in these communities. It is necessary to undertake more detailed research focusing on this topic in order to determine the overall impact of this new employment avenue on the urban poor in Sri Lanka. Here an attempt is made to identify some of the relevant factors.

To consider its positive outcomes first, this new employment avenue has enabled a segment of the urban poor to achieve some degree of upward social mobility within their own communities and, to some extent, within the larger urban society in Sri Lanka. The incomes from Middle-East jobs have been utilized mainly for housing improvements. In some rare instances, income from this avenue has been used to provide qualitatively better education for their children. There are a few instances where foreign earnings have been used to establish successful family enterprises. The urban poor, the women in particular, tend to view Middle-East employment as the only avenue open to them for escaping poverty. The structure of the affected families too has undergone some degree of change due to Middle-East employment. Earlier, males were the principal money earners within each household. The females worked hard but their contribution to family income was comparatively low. Now with the female economic contribution suddenly enhanced, she wields considerable economic power within the household. This could eventually lead to a weakening of male domination in slum and shanty communities. It is too early to say whether this new employment avenue will lead to any long-term improvement in the status of women in these communities, but the greater participation of women in foreign employment is sure to produce some lasting effect on the structure of the family in watta communities.

Yet the tendency among the females to seek foreign employment is much more pronounced in Colombo than in other cities. Jude Mawatha, which is situated close to downtown Colombo, records the highest percentage of female workers in foreign employment, followed by Swarna Mawatha, a shanty community on the edge of Colombo, Kamachchode in Negombo and Soyza Lane in Kandy.

On the negative side, many returnees from the Middle East are inclined to invest in luxury consumer durables like audio equipment, television sets etc. rather than in income generating activities per se. There are several instances where the husbands of the Middle-East workers squandered remittances from abroad by heavy involvement in drinking, gambling and other

TABLE 3.3

SECTORAL DISTRIBUTION OF WORKERS IN JUDE MAWATHA
BY SEX AND OCCUPATIONAL CATEGORY
(percentages)

Employment	Formal Sector			Informal Sector			Grand Total
	Male	Female	Total	Male	Female	Total	
Labor (Total)	59.1	0	56.6	53.5	0	31.8	38.2
Itinerant Day Laborer	0	0	0	30.2	0	17.9	13.8
Casual Laborer	36.4	0	34.8	2.3	0	1.4	9.6
Sanitary Laborer	0	0	0	0	0	0	0
Skilled Worker	22.7	0	21.8	21.0	0	12.5	14.8
Trade (Total)	0	0	0	9.3	10.4	9.7	7.2
Boutique/Shop Asst.	0	0	0	0	0	0	0
Pavement Hawker-Mobile	0	0	0	2.3	10.4	5.5	4.2
Pavement Hawker-Fixed	0	0	0	0	0	0	0
Boutique Keeper	0	0	0	2.3	0	1.4	1.0
Market Trader	0	0	0	2.3	0	1.4	1.0
Illicit Selling	0	0	0	2.3	0	1.4	1.0
Other	0	0	0	0	0	0	0
Domestic Servants (Total)	0	0	0	9.3	69.0	33.3	25.4
Employed Locally	0	0	0	0	0	0	0
Employed Abroad	0	0	0	9.3	69.0	33.3	25.4

TABLE 3.3 Continued.

Employment	Formal Sector			Informal Sector			Grand Total
	Male	Female	Total	Male	Female	Total	
Services (Total)	40.9	100.0	43.4	27.9	20.6	25.2	29.2
Clerk/Technician	0	0	0	2.3	3.4	2.8	2.1
Forces/Security Guard	9.1	0	8.7	0	0	0	2.1
Driver	0	0	0	16.4	0	9.9	7.3
Tailor/Machinist	0	100.0	4.3	2.3	10.4	5.5	5.2
Cook	0	0	0	2.3	0	1.4	1.0
Tourist Guide	0	0	0	2.3	0	1.4	1.0
Waiter/Hotel Servant	0	0	0	0	0	0	0
Transport Worker	0	0	0	2.3	3.4	2.8	2.1
Other	31.8	0	30.4	0	3.4	1.4	8.4
Other (Total)	0	0	0	0	0	0	0
Junk Dealer	0	0	0	0	0	0	0
Fisherman	0	0	0	0	0	0	0
Prostitute	0	0	0	0	0	0	0
Betting	0	0	0	0	0	0	0
Money Lender	0	0	0	0	0	0	0
Miscellaneous	0	0	0	0	0	0	0
GRAND TOTAL SAMPLE SIZE	100.0 22	100.0 1	100.0 23	100.0 43	100.0 29	100.0 72	100.0 95
TOTAL SECTOR-WISE	23 (24.2%)			72 (75.8%)			

vices. In a few cases in Jude Mawatha Middle-East employment led to marital disputes and finally the breakup of the families concerned. The children in particular tend to be neglected socially, psychologically and physically when their mothers are away for long periods of time. Some women who became disgusted with their experience in the Middle East returned home of their own accord months before their employment contracts expired.

While the negative aspects noted in the preceding paragraph cannot be overlooked, we must not loose sight of the significance of Middle-East job opportunities for the urban poor in Sri Lanka. In a context where employment opportunities available for them locally are highly restricted and hopelessly unremunerative, their attraction for this new avenue of employment is by no means surprising. It is important to bear in mind that despite the many hardships they go through in utilizing this avenue of employment, as evident from the present study, the urban poor continue to see it as a way out. Hence, future efforts should be directed towards minimizing its negative effects and maximizing the positive advantages derived from it by the inhabitants of the watta communities, the women in particular. Also this employment avenue signifies that the watta-dwellers, while primarily dependent on the informal sector, are directly linked with the world economy.

INTER-COMMUNITY DIFFERENCES IN EMPLOYMENT PATTERN

So far we examined the overall employment pattern in the four communities studied. As there are important differences among these communities in regard to their employment pattern, we will now consider some specific features of the employment pattern in each community.

Jude Mawatha

According to Table 3.3, out of a total working population of 95 in Jude Mawatha, 23 or 24.3 percent are employed in the formal sector and the remaining 75.7 percent are connected with the informal sector. The relatively high significance of the formal sector in Jude Mawatha is due to the fact that the community is situated in the vicinity of the Colombo Port and the related warehouses and processing plants, where some of the community members are employed mostly as manual laborers.

It is also important to note that some 25 percent of all workers in this community and as much as 69 percent of all women employed in the informal sector are working in the Middle East. This in turn is related to the fact that there are several foreign employment agencies within easy access to Jude Mawatha. Both the sources of information about foreign employment and the relevant facilities, including the passport office and airline offices, are easily accessible to those in Jude Mawatha.

Finally, pavement hawking and related commercial activities are only marginally important in Jude Mawatha even though it is situated not far from Pettah, a leading commercial center in Colombo. However, due to its proximity to the Colombo Port, smuggling is of considerable importance in this community and may be disguised as pavement hawking or some other legitimate business activity.

Swarna Mawatha

As evident from Table 3.4, in Swarna Mawatha the formal sector accounts for only 21.6 percent of the workers as against 78.4 percent of the workers employed in the informal sector. Many of the formal sector workers are employed as casual laborers mostly

81

TABLE 3.4

SECTORAL DISTRIBUTION OF WORKERS IN SWARNA MAWATHA
BY SEX AND EMPLOYMENT CATEGORY
(Percentages)

Employment	Formal Sector			Informal Sector			Grand Total
	Male	Female	Total	Male	Female	Total	
Labor (Total)	83.3	0	83.3	55.5	12.2	39.0	48.6
Itinerant Day Laborer	0	0	0	29.6	6.1	20.7	16.2
Casual Laborer	70.8	0	70.8	1.8	0	1.1	16.2
Sanitary Laborer	4.2	0	4.2	0	6.1	2.3	2.7
Skilled Worker	8.3	0	8.3	24.1	0	14.9	13.5
Trade (Total)	0	0	0	13.0	3.0	8.4	7.3
Boutique/Shop Asst.	0	0	0	3.8	0	2.8	1.8
Pavement Hawker-Mobile	0	0	0	1.8	0	1.1	1.0
Pavement hawker-Fixed	0	0	0	0	0	0	0
Boutique Keeper	0	0	0	0	0	0	0
Market Trader	0	0	0	0	0	0	0
Illicit Selling	0	0	0	1.8	3.0	1.1	1.8
Other	0	0	0	5.6	0	3.4	2.7
Domestic Servants (Total)	0	0	0	3.6	84.8	34.5	27.0
Employed Locally	0	0	0	1.8	51.5	20.7	16.2
Employed Abroad	0	0	0	1.8	33.3	13.8	10.8

TABLE 3.4 Continued.

Employment	Formal Sector			Informal Sector			Grand Total
	Male	Female	Total	Male	Female	Total	
Services (Total)	16.7	0	16.7	24.3	0	16.0	15.0
Clerk/Technician	0	0	0	0	0	0	0
Forces/Security Guard	4.2	0	4.2	0	0	0	0
Driver	4.2	0	4.2	5.3	0	3.4	2.6
Tailor/Machinist	0	0	0	3.4	0	2.3	1.7
Cook	0	0	0	15.6	0	10.3	8.1
Tourist Guide	0	0	0	0	0	0	0
Waiter/Hotel Servant	0	0	0	0	0	0	0
Transport Worker	0	0	0	0	0	0	0
Other	8.3	0	8.3	0	0	0	2.6
Other (Total)	0	0	0	3.6	0	2.1	2.0
Junk Dealer	0	0	0	1.8	0	1.1	1.0
Fisherman	0	0	0	0	0	0	0
Prostitute	0	0	0	0	0	0	0
Betting	0	0	0	0	0	0	0
Money Lender	0	0	0	1.8	0	1.1	1.0
Miscellaneous	0	0	0	0	0	0	0
GRAND TOTAL	100.0	100.0	100.0	100.0	100.0	100.0	100.0
SAMPLE SIZE	24	0	24	54	33	87	111
TOTAL SECTOR-WISE	43 (21.6%)			87 (78.4%)			

in the nearby Wellawatta Weaving Mills. There are also a few skilled laborers, sanitary laborers, security guards and drivers employed in the formal sector. Not a single woman from this community is employed in the formal sector.

It is quite significant that nearly 85 percent of all working women in Swarna Mawatha are employed as domestic servants. As Swarna Mawatha is located adjacent to a middle-class residential area, women from Swarna Mawatha find it easy to secure work as domestic helpers in nearby middle-class homes; often they come back to their own homes after a day's work in these middle-class houses. There are also a number of men from Swarna Mawatha employed as cooks, mostly in the homes of foreign diplomats. Both male and female domestic servants in Swarna Mawatha come mostly from among the Indian Tamils in this community.

In a way, as far as those in Swarna Mawatha are concerned, employment opportunities in the Middle East have grown out of their background as domestic helpers in local middle-class homes. The access to foreign employment agencies and other facilities relevant to Middle-East employment is not so important in Swarna Mawatha. As in Jude Mawatha, a relatively few people from Swarna Mawatha are engaged in petty trade.

Soyza Lane

No one from Soyza Lane is employed in the formal sector. Since this community is situated in the heart of Kandy town, it serves as a focus for informal sector activities in the town. The principal economic activity in Soyza Lane is petty trade, followed by laboring jobs, service occupations and several illegal operations (see Table 3.5).

For the most part Soyza Lane serves as a center of pavement hawking in Kandy. The community members have control over strategically important selling points within the city center. While some women operate as betel sellers in some fixed locations in the city, some of the men go out and sell pineapples, ice cream, fancy goods, cannabis (ganja) and various other items. When the police or municipal authorities raid illegal pavement operations, those from Soyza Lane often manage to quickly run back to their homes with their merchandise safely in their hands. Some pavement hawkers from outside the community keep their stocks in houses in Soyza Lane because of the strategic commercial advantage of the location of this community.

A considerable number of men from Soyza Lane work as porters (natami) in the nearby bus stand, railway station and the market. The livelihood of the porters too depend heavily on their ability to be in the right place at the right time.

Finally, Soyza Lane serves as a center of various illegal operations in town, including prostitution, pick pocketing, drug trafficking and distribution of illicit liquor. A considerable number of women in this community depend heavily on prostitution and other unlawful activities for their livelihood (for details see Silva, 1985). For the most part the community provides protection and support as well as a social identity to those engaged in illicit operations of one kind or another, an essential component of the urban informal sector. The various criminal elements in the community tend to operate jointly. On the whole the livelihood of those in Soyza Lane is intricately linked with the bus stand, the railway station, the market and, above all, the busy city streets surrounding this community. The community's persistent struggle to remain in the city center in turn can be understood against the above background.

TABLE 3.5

SECTORAL DISTRIBUTION OF WORKERS IN SOYZA LANE
BY SEX AND EMPLOYMENT CATEGORY
(Percentages)

Employment	Formal Sector			Informal Sector			Grand Total
	Male	Female	Total	Male	Female	Total	
Labor (Total)	0	0	0	28.8	38.4	31.0	31.0
Itinerant Day Laborer	0	0	0	28.8	30.7	29.3	29.3
Casual Laborer	0	0	0	0	0	0	0
Sanitary Laborer	0	0	0	0	0	0	0
Skilled Worker	0	0	0	0	7.7	1.7	1.7
Trade (Total)	0	0	0	46.8	30.8	43.1	43.1
Boutique/Shop Asst.	0	0	0	6.7	0	5.2	5.2
Pavement Hawker-Mobile	0	0	0	6.7	15.4	8.6	8.6
Pavement Hawker-Fixed	0	0	0	0	0	0	0
Boutique Keeper	0	0	0	17.8	0	13.8	13.8
Market Trader	0	0	0	0	0	0	0
Illicit Selling	0	0	0	6.7	15.4	8.6	8.6
Other	0	0	0	8.9	0	6.9	6.9
Domestic Servants (Total)	0	0	0	2.2	0	1.7	1.7
Employed Locally	0	0	0	0	0	0	0
Employed Abroad	0	0	0	2.2	0	1.7	1.7

TABLE 3.5 Continued.

Employment	Formal Sector			Informal Sector			Grand Total
	Male	Female	Total	Male	Female	Total	
Services (Total)	0	0	0	17.8	7.7	15.5	15.5
Clerk/Technician	0	0	0	8.9	0	6.9	6.9
Forces/Security Guard	0	0	0	0	0	0	0
Driver	0	0	0	0	0	0	0
Tailor/Machinist	0	0	0	0	0	0	0
Cook	0	0	0	0	7.7	1.7	1.7
Tourist Guide	0	0	0	0	0	0	0
Waiter/Hotel Servant	0	0	0	8.9	0	6.9	6.9
Transport Worker	0	0	0	0	0	0	0
Other	0	0	0	0	0	0	0
Other (Total)	0	0	0	4.4	23.1	8.5	8.5
Junk Dealer	0	0	0	0	7.7	1.7	1.7
Fisherman	0	0	0	0	0	0	0
Prostitute	0	0	0	0	15.4	3.4	3.4
Betting	0	0	0	0	0	0	0
Money Lender	0	0	0	4.4	0	3.4	3.4
Miscellaneous	0	0	0	0	0	0	0
GRAND TOTAL	0	0	0	100.0	100.0	100.0	100.0
SAMPLE SIZE	0	0	0	45	13	58	58
TOTAL SECTOR-WISE	0			58 (100.0%)			

TABLE 3.6

SECTORAL DISTRIBUTION OF WORKERS IN KAMACHCHODE
BY SEX AND OCCUPATIONAL CATEGORY
(Percentages)

Employment	Formal Sector			Informal Sector			Grand Total
	Male	Female	Total	Male	Female	Total	
Labor (Total)	50.0	16.7	41.1	9.9	17.8	12.6	17.0
Itinerant Day Laborer	0	0	0	0	17.8	5.9	5.0
Casual Laborer	25.0	0	18.3	5.5	0	3.7	5.7
Sanitary Laborer	0	16.7	4.5	0	0	0	1.3
Skilled Worker	25.0	0	18.3	4.4	0	3.0	5.0
Trade (Total)	12.4	33.3	18.1	48.9	42.3	46.7	42.4
Boutique/Shop Asst	6.2	0	4.5	7.8	0	5.2	5.0
Pavement Hawker-Mobile	0	0	0	6.7	13.4	8.9	7.6
Pavement Hawker-Fixed	0	0	0	0	0	0	0
Boutique Keeper	0	0	0	1.1	0	0.7	0.6
Market Trader	0	0	0	12.2	20.0	14.8	12.7
Illicit Selling	0	0	0	1.1	6.7	3.0	2.5
Other	6.2	33.3	13.6	20.0	2.2	14.1	14.0
Domestic Servants (Total)	0	0	0	1.1	19.9	7.4	6.3
Employed Locally	0	0	0	0	2.2	0.7	0.6
Employed Abroad	0	0	0	1.1	17.7	6.7	5.7

TABLE 3.6 Continued.

Employment	Formal Sector			Informal Sector			Grand Total
	Male	Female	Total	Male	Female	Total	
Services (Total)	37.6	50.0	40.8	7.9	17.8	11.0	15.2
Clerk/Technician	6.2	0	4.5	0	0	0	0.6
Forces/Security Guard	6.3	0	4.5	0	0	0	0.6
Driver	0	0	0	3.3	0	2.2	2.0
Tailor/Machinist	6.3	50.0	18.3	0	8.9	3.0	5.0
Cook	6.3	0	4.5	0	0	0	0.6
Tourist Guide	0	0	0	0	0	0	0
Waiter/Hotel Servant	0	0	0	0	0	0	0
Transport Worker	6.2	0	4.5	0	0	0	0.6
Other	6.3	0	4.5	4.6	8.9	5.8	5.8
Other (Total)	0	0	0	32.2	2.2	22.3	19.1
Junk Dealer	0	0	0	0	0	0	0
Fisherman	0	0	0	32.2	2.2	22.3	19.1
Prostitute	0	0	0	0	0	0	0
Betting	0	0	0	0	0	0	0
Money Lender	0	0	0	0	0	0	0
Miscellaneous	0	0	0	0	0	0	0
GRAND TOTAL	100.0	100.0	100.0	100.0	100.0	100.0	100.0
SAMPLE SIZE	16	6	22	90	45	135	157
TOTAL SECTOR-WISE	22 (14.0%)			135 (86.0%)			

Kamachchode

In Kamachchode, too, the economy is by and large
dominated by the informal sector, with only 14 percent
of the economically active engaged in the formal
sector (see Table 3.6). As in the other three communities the employment pattern in Kamachchode is
heavily influenced by its physical location. The
community is situated on the Negombo beach, close to
the city center and the Old Fish Market. Thus the
employment pattern in Kamachchode is much influenced
by the sea and the nearby market place.

Some 19 percent of all workers in Kamachchode are
employed as fishermen by fish Mudalalies [2] outside
the community who own mechanized fishing boats and the
required fishing gear. These fishermen are given a
share of the catch by their employers.

Some of the other community members, mostly wives
of fishermen, take part in the selling of fish either
as market traders or hawkers, comprising another 20
percent of all workers in Kamachchode. Thus nearly 40
percent of the economically active in Kamachchode are
directly or indirectly connected with the fish
industry.

For the most part the remaining income earners are
engaged in laboring jobs or service occupations mainly
in Negombo town. Some men and a few women from
Kamachchode are employed in the garment factories
situated in the Katunayaka export processing zone.
Nearly six percent of the economically active are
currently working in the Middle East.

Thus the employment pattern in each community is
influenced largely by its location and environment.
Each community tends to have a predominant subsistence
base whether it is laboring opportunities in Jude
Mawatha and Swarna Mawatha, pavement hawking in Soyza

Lane or fishing in Kamachchode. Jude Mawatha has the highest proportion of its workers in the formal sector followed by Swarna Mawatha and Kamachchode. Soyza Lane is more or less completely cut off from the formal sector in the city.

PLACE OF RESIDENCE AND EMPLOYMENT

We have already seen that the pattern of employment in each community is heavily influenced by its location. We can explore this question further by examining the relationship between place of residence and place of work among the watta-dwellers. The relevant data are presented in Table 3.7.

TABLE   3.7

DISTANCE TO PLACE OF WORK

Distance	Total	Percentage
Within the community	70	16.6
Walking distance	122	28.9
Less than 1 mile	19	4.5
1 - 2 miles	30	7.1
2 - 5 miles	78	18.5
More than 5 miles	55	13.0
Foreign employment	46	10.9
No information	2	0.5
Total	422	100.0

Table 3.7 shows that 45.5 percent of the working population live in close proximity to their usual place of work. However, it is evident that another 50 percent of the sample have their working places one mile or more away from their place of residence. Thus the distance to work does not appear to be the sole

factor that determines one's place of residence. In a situation where public transport services are both cheap and efficient, distance to work itself may not be as important as ready availability of public transport to required places of work. In any case, being itinerant day laborers or casual laborers, many of the watta residents do not have fixed places of employment and, irrespective of the distance, they must travel to places where employment opportunities are available.

It is possible that while the first generation of watta residents chose to live in the respective locations due to their convenience and proximity to places of employment, the subsequent generations were less successful in obtaining employment close to their homes. In this regard it is important to examine the reasons given by heads of households for choosing the present place of residence.

TABLE 3.8

THE REASON FOR CHOOSING THE PRESENT PLACE
OF RESIDENCE

Reason	f	Percentage
Proximity to work	17	8.0
Convenience to find jobs	11	5.1
Education of children	8	3.7
Marriage	50	23.1
Availability of kinsmen	14	6.4
Other reasons	73	33.7
Not applicable/No information	43	20.0
Total	216	100.0

According to Table 3.8, only 13 percent of household heads chose their present places of residence because of proximity to employment per se. Social links arising from marriage and availability of kinsmen appear to have been of greater importance in their choice of residential locations. Such social ties, however, may be seen as an avenue for obtaining access to certain income earning opportunities, especially in the informal sector. This in turn shows the interplay of social and economic processes in watta communities.

LEVEL OF UNEMPLOYMENT

While any systematic inquiry into unemployment and underemployment in watta communities was beyond the scope of the present study, some evidence concerning level of unemployment in the four study communities can be considered here.

A total of 45.8 percent of the work force in the four communities are reported to be unemployed (see Table 3.9). The unemployment rate for females is 67.3 percent as against 24.4 percent for males. This disparity is partly due to the inclusion of housewives among the unemployed. However, as many housewives too are likely to work given the opportunity, we may conclude that the watta women have a much higher rate of unemployment compared to their menfolk. The highest rate of unemployment is in Jude Mawatha, followed by Kamachchode and Soyza Lane.

There appears to be more than full employment among males in Swarna Mawatha. This may be due to the fact that underaged boys in this community quite frequently work. While male unemployment is quite variable, female unemployment remains above 60 percent in all four communities. Thus, despite Middle-East employment, the employment opportunities for watta women remain highly restricted.

TABLE   3.9

LEVEL OF UNEMPLOYMENT BY COMMUNITY AND SEX

Name of Community	Category		
	Total Work force	Total Employed	Percentage Unemployed
Jude Mawatha			
Male	101	65	35.6
Female	99	30	69.7
Total	200	95	52.5
Swarna Mawatha			
Male	74	78	-5.4
Female	88	33	62.5
Total	162	111	31.5
Soyza Lane			
Male	59	45	23.7
Female	44	13	70.5
Total	103	58	43.7
Kamachchode			
Male	155	106	31.6
Female	157	51	67.5
Total	312	157	49.7
All			
Male	389	294	24.4
Female	388	127	67.3
Total	777	421	45.8

INCOME AND EXPENDITURE PATTERN

In the household survey the respondents were asked to describe average household income per month from different sources of income, including food stamps. There was some reluctance to answer this question on the part of certain households. Moreover, the investigators found that the income figures given by certain households were completely unreliable. Where the investigators encountered such difficulties they were instructed to estimate the average monthly income of the relevant households on the basis of their responses to the employment questions. This procedure was not entirely satisfactory, but we could not find a better way of establishing the income levels of the relevant households.

The income data obtained through the above procedure are given in Table 3.10. Thus the average household income per month for the whole sample is Rs.1,990 (US$ 66.30) [3]. This may seem rather high for a low-income population, but the inflow of foreign earnings to a substantial number of households is a major cause of the relatively inflated income levels in these communities. It is also evident that income variation within each of these communities is quite high. When all four communities are taken together 15.4 percent of the households have a mean monthly income of less than Rs.800, which was defined by UNICEF as poverty line for Sri Lanka in 1986 [4]. On the other hand, 17.1 percent of the households have an average monthly income of over Rs.3,200. The wide gap in income levels is also reflected in the high standard deviation on income levels.

The inter-community variation in income levels is also quite marked. The highest average monthly income of Rs.2,473 is found in Jude Mawatha, followed by Rs. 2,190 for Kamachchode, Rs.1,839 for Swarna Mawatha and Rs.1,460 for Soyza Lane. It is important to note that

TABLE 3.10

DISTRIBUTION OF HOUSEHOLDS ACCORDING TO AVERAGE INCOME

Average Monthly Income Rs.	COMMUNITY									
	JM		SM		SL		KM		ALL	
	f	%	f	%	f	%	f	%	f	%
0 - 399	0	0	1	2.0	1	3.0	0	0	2	1.0
400 - 799	8	16.4	8	15.7	10	30.3	5	6.0	31	14.4
800 - 1,599	15	30.6	26	50.9	11	33.4	33	39.8	85	39.3
1,600 - 3,199	11	22.4	8	15.7	10	30.3	32	38.5	61	28.2
3,200 & Above	15	30.6	8	15.7	1	3.0	13	15.7	37	17.1
Total	49	100.0	51	100.0	33	100.0	83	100.0	216	100.0
Average	2,473/=		1,839/=		1,460/=		2,190/=		1,990/=	
Standard Deviation	1,668/=		1,402/=		964/=		1,283		1,329/=	

both Jude Mawatha and Kamachchode, the communities
with a higher average income have large numbers of
people working in the Middle East while Soyza Lane,
with the lowest average income reportedly has only one
person currently employed in the Middle East. Further,
it can be seen that the proportion of households in
the highest income group is highest in Jude Mawatha
which has benefited most from employment opportunities
in the Middle East. Thus remittances from abroad are
an important factor in inter-community variations in
income levels as regards the urban poor.

Table 3.11 provides a classification of households
according to their main source of income.

TABLE 3.11

DISTRIBUTION OF HOUSEHOLDS ACCORDING TO
MAIN SOURCE OF INCOME

Main Source of Income	Number of Households	Percentage
Employment	183	84.8
Food Stamps	7	3.1
Public Charity & Aid	9	4.1
Property & Investments	17	8.0
Total	216	100.0

A vast majority of urban low-income households
(84.8%) earn a living through selling their labor
power. Only 7 percent of the households earn their
living from property and investments of some sort.
About 7 percent of the households depend mainly on
food stamps or charities.

An important feature of the expenditure pattern of low-income households anywhere in the world is that a very high proportion of their total expenditure is spent on the food bill. The Marga study referred to earlier also highlighted this point. The findings of the present study confirm this pattern. According to Table 3.12, on the average, 67.6 percent of the total expenditure of a household is spent on the food bill. The other household expenditure items are not very significant relative to the food bill. However, it is quite significant that 8 percent of their total expenditure is spent on alcohol, betel and smoking. This has important implications for both their economic well-being and health status. They also spend a considerable amount on fuel.

TABLE 3.12

PERCENTAGE DISTRIBUTION OF AVERAGE HOUSEHOLD EXPENDITURE ACCORDING TO ITEM OF EXPENDITURE

Item of Expenditure	Percentage
Food	67.6
Rent/Loan Repayment	2.2
Fuel	7.0
Education of Children	4.8
Alcohol, Betel and Smoking	8.0
Health	3.6
Recreation	1.8
Other	5.0
Total	100.0

Two other important features of urban poverty are lack of possession of any capital assets and heavy indebtedness. Data concerning indebtedness are given in Table 3.13.

TABLE 3.13

PERCENTAGE DISTRIBUTION OF HOUSEHOLDS ACCORDING TO THE
AMOUNT OF MONEY INDEBTED

Household Debts Rs.	COMMUNITY									
	JM		SM		SL		KM		ALL	
	f	%	f	%	f	%	f	%	f	%
No loan taken	35	71.4	14	27.4	14	42.4	53	63.8	116	53.7
0 - 399	5	10.2	6	11.8	8	24.2	6	7.2	25	11.6
400 - 799	2	4.1	5	9.8	4	12.1	3	3.6	14	6.5
800 - 1,599	0	0	10	19.6	3	9.1	3	3.6	16	7.4
1,600 - 3,199	2	4.1	9	17.6	2	6.1	3	3.6	16	7.4
3,200 - 6,399	2	4.1	2	4.0	2	6.1	6	7.2	12	5.6
6,400 & Above	3	6.1	5	9.8	0	0	9	11.0	17	7.8
Total	49	100.0	51	100.0	33	100.0	83	100.0	216	100.0
Average	926/=		1,870/=		667/=		1,554/=		1,254/=	
Standard Deviation	2,470/=		2,816/=		1,238/=		3,104/=		2,407/=	

It is evident that the households in the sample have an average indebtedness of Rs.1,254. The highest average household indebtedness of Rs.1,870 is in Swarna Mawatha followed by Rs.1,554 for Kamachchode, Rs.926 for Jude Mawatha and Rs.667 for Soyza Lane.

A kind of informal social arrangement for raising credit known as the seettu system exists, especially among women, in all four communities studied. Under this system each partner contributes a fixed sum of money each month towards a collective fund, and the total collection is handed over to one partner at a time, making sure that the total collection rotates among all partners over a given period of time. The seettu system is seen as an effective mutual-aid arrangement, whereby the low-income households raise a sizable sum of money from time to time for the purchase of jewelry, sewing machines etc. or for various other purposes. The significance of the seettu system for urban low-income neighborhoods is evidenced by the fact that one of the four communities studied, Jude Mawatha, was formerly known as Seettu Petti Watta, meaning a watta founded by an organizer of a seettu arrangement [5].

SUMMARY AND CONCLUSION

By and large the economic activities of the urban poor are linked with the informal sector. Any effort to increase their participation within the formal sector may not be realistic in the short run in view of the low educational levels and the lack of capital among them. In this context any realistic strategy for improving the economy of the urban poor must largely focus on ways and means of strengthening the informal sector. Removal of legal restrictions against important informal sector activities such as pavement hawking; provision of improved credit facilities for those engaged in small business; provision of required management and vocational training; promotion of cooperative action among informal sector workers, like load carriers, construction workers and fishermen; and technical support like provision of push carts to load carriers, are some of the possibilities for improving the labor absorption capacity, profitability and productivity of the informal sector.

The benefits of Middle-East employment could be improved further by initiating a program of guidance and counselling addressed especially to those who return from Middle-East employment. There is also some scope for developing the skills of potential applicants for Middle-East employment from these communities. As female unemployment is particularly acute in these communities steps must be taken to improve employment opportunities for women. Avenues for improving the income levels of the poorer groups in these communities must be explored, along with strategies for reducing household expenditure on alcohol, betel and smoking.

NOTES

1. This findings is supported by other recent studies in watta communities. For instance, see Wantawin (1982).

2. A local term for traders and entrepreneurs.

3. This compares with the average monthly household expenditure of Rs.1,956 (US$ 65.20). At the time of fieldwork the prevailing exchange rate was 1 US$ = Sri Lanka Rupees 30.00.

4. See, for instance, UNICEF 1987, p.2.

5. For details please see Chapter Two.

CHAPTER FOUR

SOCIAL ORGANIZATION

To what extent is there an orderly social life in watta communities? What factors contribute to any prevailing social order in these communities? To what extent can the watta-dwellers be described as rootless, marginal and alienated? What are the distinctive characteristics of watta communities as against other types of urban and rural communities in Sri Lanka? Is there any difference in social organization between inner-city slums and peripheral shanty communities? How does the social life in these communities relate to the larger society of Sri Lanka? These are some of the issues addressed in this chapter.

The various parameters of the social organization in watta communities are discussed below.

WATTA AS A COMMUNITY

As shown in Chapter Two each watta is a well-defined neighborhood with clear boundaries, whether they are streets, footpaths, waterways or property boundaries of some kind. A watta, however, is not merely a well-defined locality occupied by a collection of people with some common socio-economic characteristics. It may also be viewed as a community of people occupying a common locality and bound together through a network of relationships. The inhabitants of each watta refer to their locale by terms such as <u>ape watta</u> (our neighborhood) or <u>ape kalla</u> (our block) and refer to themselves as a community by phrases like me watte minissu (people of this watta), ape watte kattiya (those of our watta) etc. Within each watta there is intense social interaction centering around regular meeting places, whether they are private houses, boutiques, water taps or other public places like nearby playgrounds. Within a watta each inhabitant is personally known to every other inhabitant; unknown outsiders are immediately spotted by the local inhabitants and an explanation is directly or indirectly sought from such visitors.

The communal use of water taps, toilets and other public utilities is one of several factors that necessitate a pervasive community outlook in the day-to-day social life in the wattas. The inhabitants of a watta have many other shared interests including a constant need to deal with threats from outside. Even where the formal community-wide organizations are inactive or non-existent, the entire community is readily mobilized, especially when it faces a threat from the outside. As will be shown, the neighborhood ties within each community are often reinforced through kinship, caste and ethnic bonds. Further, as noted earlier, a majority of households in each watta, far from being transient, are longstanding inhabitants with strong roots in the respective localities.

There is a broad pattern of mutual help and reciprocity within each watta. Items of exchange include food, clothing, jewelry and household appliances. Members of one household often utilize sleeping space in neighboring households to accommodate visitors or even additional family members. TVs, sewing machines, irons, bicycles, though privately owned, are normally accessible to friends, neighbors and kinsmen of their owners. In crisis situations like illness, death or even domestic disputes, neighbors readily intervene without paying regard to the caste or ethnic identity of the people concerned. Communal fund raising for funerals, religious festivities and other such purposes is also common. Invariably there is mutual help in activities such as thatching of houses.

The mutual concern among neighbors and their curiosity for one another are reinforced by the sheer physical proximity of housing units within a watta. Nothing can remain highly confidential or personal given the particular nature of the neighborhoods. In addition, gossip and rumor, important social controls in watta communities, add to the vigorousness of community norms.

As a general rule the degree of solidarity within a watta community appears to be inversely related to its size, extent of caste and ethnic heterogeneity and the degree of income differentiation within it. Within each watta there are frequent quarrels over use of public water taps, latrines and other such public utilities. Conflicts between landlords and tenants and conflicts over women are also common. There were instances of sorcery allegations against neighbors or kinsmen in Swarna Mawatha and Kamachchode. In Soyza Lane there was an ongoing battle between those earning their livelihood from vices of some kind and a few people in the community who were opposed to such activities and determined to cleanse the community of its many vices with a view to achieving some degree of self-respect. There is, however, concerted effort within each watta to resolve the various internal conflicts amicably without resorting to any outside agencies. When fights do break out among community people there are neutral parties who intervene and break up the fights, sometimes using sheer physical strength.

GENDER

Relations between men and women constitute a key aspect of the social organization in the wattas. The high regard for masculinity may be seen as a dominant

105

social value among the watta-dwellers. One's physical
strength demonstrated in brawls and sporting activities is critical for achieving leadership in male peer
groups, irrespective of age. Many of the community
leaders too are strongly-built people with aggressive
qualities. The popularity of body-building, karate and
football among men also signifies their respect for
masculinity.

The watta women, however, are not necessarily
submissive in their relations with men. In contrast,
in Kamachchode where most men spend a good part of
their time at sea fishing, women play a prominent role
both in the domestic sphere and in community affairs.
Similarly, women in Soyza Lane operate as a frontline
defense against threats from the police, municipality
or any other hostile group from outside.

As for household responsibilities, men are often
less concerned about the welfare of their families
compared to women. The family units in watta communities may be generally described as "mother-
centered". Nearly 18 percent of all households in the
four study communities are female-headed, that is to
say headed by women who are widowed, separated or
divorced from their husbands. Even in other households
the mother usually serves as the core of the family,
with fathers often shying away from their parental
responsibilities. The household responsibilities of
women increase with the increase in family size. It is
common for the mother to get help from her daughters,
especially in the care of their younger siblings. Some
instances of wife beating were reported in each of the
four communities studied. Desertions by husbands were
quite frequent. There were also a few reported
instances of incestuous sexual advances by step-
fathers on step-daughters. Possibly as an outcome of
these conditions, mental stress as manifested in
spirit possessions, aggressiveness and even suicide

attempts appeared to be more frequent among watta women as compared to their male counterparts.

PEER GROUPS

The peer groups formed on the basis of sex and age play a significant role in watta communities. The important peer groups among males and females in different age groups are listed in Table 4.1.

TABLE 4.1

A CLASSIFICATION OF PEER GROUPS
AMONG THE WATTA-DWELLERS

| Age Group | Type of Peer Group | |
	Male	Female
2 - 5	Play group	Play group
6 - 14	Play group School Gang	Play group School Gang
15 - 30	Gang Sports club Work team	Water tap users Interest group Work team
31 - 60	Work team Interest group	Water tap users Interest group
Over 60	Interest group	Interest group

Pre-school children in neighboring households tend to interact closely with one another in the form of play groups. At this age boys and girls play with one another quite freely. "Hide and Seek" and hopscotch are popular among watta children in this age group. Often their play activities spread to any open space in between houses or even to nearby footpaths and lanes.

After six years of age boys and girls tend to form separate peer groups. Among boys in the 6-14 age group, in addition to play groups, school and gang affiliations become important bases for peer group activity. Membership in these groups tends to overlap. These older boys prefer to play football [1], elle (a local game similar to baseball) and cricket. Nearby playgrounds, parks or beaches are commonly used for playing these games. For school-going children in watta communities their school affiliation is significant both as a means of extra-community identity and as a basis for interaction with peers from a wider area. There are gangs particularly among school dropouts in a watta community. A gang is usually led by an older boy with proven physical strength.

Each gang tends to have a well-defined territory, whether it is a section of a watta neighborhood, a complete watta or a cluster of neighboring watta. Gang rivalries among those of nearby wattas are common. The members of a gang normally have more than one interest in common. As was pointed out by Jayasooriya and Kariyawasam (1958) in an earlier study, these juvenile gangs are inclined to get into delinquent practices like smoking, petty theft or even drug peddling. More often, however, the members of a juvenile gang merely enjoy themselves collectively through playing games, movie going or simply wandering in the city.

Peer groups among males in the 15-30 age group consist of work teams, sports clubs and gangs. Load carriers (natami) and hawkers in Soyza Lane, fishermen in Kamachchode and some harbor workers in Jude Mawatha may be cited as good examples of peer groups formed on the basis of work. For instance, the load carriers from Soyza Lane have control over work opportunities in several fixed places in the city and they operate as a group in order to maintain that position. The sports clubs may be seen as an adult and more formalized version of play groups prevalent among those in the younger age groups. As will be elaborated in the next chapter, these clubs often bring together the various professional players in a single game.

Gangs consisting of adult males are in many ways similar to those discussed in the preceding paragraphs and may have grown out of the latter in some instances. These adult gangs, however, tend to have more advanced criminal tendencies including, in some instances, the possession and use of explosive substances. Often the local police keeps a watchful eye on the activities of these gangs. Some of the adult gangs have direct links with certain influential figures outside these communities. However, it is wrong to say that the adult gangs, where they exist, solely serve criminal ends. The zest for collective enjoyment remains important for those in adult gangs too. For instance, it is customary for the members of a certain youth gang in Jude Mawatha to take part in an annual pilgrimage to a well-known Catholic center during its festival season, get themselves drunk there and have any new members in the group tattooed by the professional tattooists who come there for the occasion.

There appears to be less peer group activity among older men and women. Only certain types of interest groups exist as exclusive peer groups among men older than 30 years. Usually these groups involve interaction among those sharing a single common interest, whether it is receipt of Public Assistance, betting on horses, drinking or any other activity.

Peer groups among females older than six years are separate from, but to some extent, parallel to male peer groups in the corresponding age ranges. Girls in the 6-14 age group usually have their own play groups and own groups based on school affiliation. In contrast to boys, girls typically play indoor games using sea shells etc. In the case of girls their transition to adulthood is marked by a puberty ceremony, which is widely celebrated in watta communities. Among the female young adults in the 15-30 age group, important peer groups are formed around the common use of water taps, wash rooms etc. and those based on shared interests such as sewing, cooking, and marketing. There are important peer groups among market women in Kamachchode, among prostitutes in Soyza Lane and among women seeking Middle-East employment in Jude Mawatha. It is important to note that no structural equivalents of sports clubs and gangs exist among females in the 15-30 age group. Watta women older than 30 years tend to have their own peer groups centered around the use of common taps and shared interests like religious observances.

On the whole the various peer groups serve as an important basis for collective action among watta-dwellers.

FAMILY AND KINSHIP

Family and kinship ties determine intra-household and, to a lesser extent, inter-household social relations among watta-dwellers. Each household within a watta is a family unit of some kind. According to their composition, watta households can be divided into the four categories given below.

1. Single parent or parentless households.
2. Nuclear families, each comprising of father, mother and children.
3. Extended families formed by the addition of one or more individual kinsmen to the nuclear family.

TABLE 4.2

HOUSEHOLD COMPOSITION

Household Category	Jude Mawatha		Swarna Mawatha		Soyza Lane		Kamach-chode		Total	
	No.	%	No.	%	No.	%	No.	%	No.	%
Single-Parent/ Parentless	11	22.5	5	9.8	11	33.3	17	20.5	44	20.4
Nuclear Family	15	30.6	25	49.0	12	36.4	25	30.1	77	35.6
Extended Family	15	30.6	14	27.5	9	27.3	29	34.9	67	31.0
Joint Family	8	16.3	7	13.7	1	3.0	12	14.5	28	13.0
Total	49	100.0	51	100.0	33	100.0	83	100.0	216	100.0

4. Joint families each comprising two or more closely related nuclear families sharing a single household.

The relative importance of each type of household is given in Table 4.2.

Nearly 45 percent of all households in the sample are either extended or joint families. The proportion of these larger kinship units varies from 30 percent in Soyza Lane to 49 percent in Kamachchode. Jude Mawatha has the highest proportion of joint families (16%), indicating that married children in this inner-city slum frequently remain in the parental households. The higher prevalence of larger family units in Jude Mawatha may be due to a greater housing scarcity in inner-city areas rather than due to the strength of kinship ties per se. The pattern in Soyza Lane, however, is quite different as it has the lowest prevalence of joint families and extended families.

Single parent or parentless households account for 20 percent of the households in the sample. In so far as these households have an incomplete kinship structure where supportive mechanisms are weak, they deserve the attention of the relevant social welfare programs. The proportion of such households vary from 10 percent in Swarna Mawatha to 33 percent in Soyza Lane. On the whole the data indicate that the slums (Jude Mawatha and Soyza Lane) have a higher proportion of broken families compared to the shanty communities, with Swarna Mawatha consisting exclusively of shanty dwellers having the lowest proportion of broken homes. This may be indicative of a higher degree of social organization in shanty communities compared to slums.

Each watta community tends to have an inner-core of households which are strongly connected through kinship ties. For instance, 24 out of the 33 households in Soyza Lane (72.7%) are linked through kinship

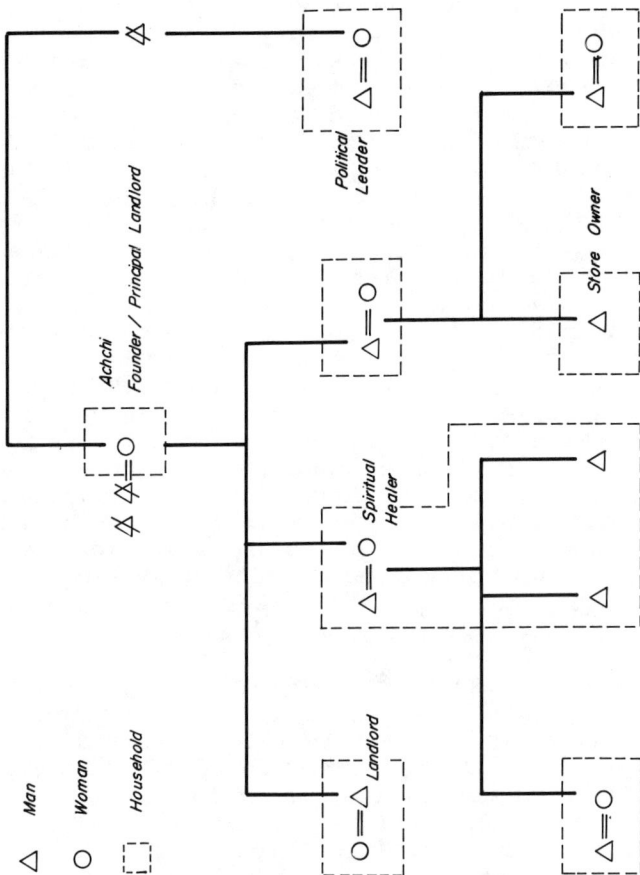

Figure 1 : THE KINSHIP NETWORK IN SWARNA MAWATHA

△ Man

○ Woman

▢ Household

ties. Similarly almost all the community leaders in Swarna Mawatha belong to eight households, all descending from one of the founders of the community (see Figure 1).

The founder of the above kin group is an 81-year-old Sinhalese woman, commonly known in the community as "Achchi" (grandmother), who, as described in Chapter Two, was also a founder of the Swarna Mawatha community. Together with her children she moved to Swarna Mawatha in 1949, having separated from her second husband who was from a nearby watta community. She came to the canal bank, cleared the site and set up a household there. Even though there were a few squatter families already living on the canal bank, Achchi was able to take control of a greater part of land on the canal bank. Later, her children got married and established their own households in various places along the canal bank. The subsequent incomers, most of whom were Indian Tamils, either purchased or rented housing lots from Achchi or from her children and put up their own shanty units to form two continuous lines of shanties along the canal bank. Achchi also permitted some of her other relatives to move into the community by providing free house sites. Apart from controlling house sites, various members of the kin group controlled political leadership, retail trade, spiritual healing and other important activities in the community.

The above example from Swarna Mawatha illustrates the importance of kinship in the formation of watta communities, as well as its role in several aspects of watta social organization, including property transmission, land tenure and leadership pattern. There is also a marked tendency towards matrilineal descent and matrilocal residence in all four communities studied. The position of Achchi (grandmother) illustrates the role of the maternal ancestor in keeping the kinship

114

unit intact. The mother-centered nature of the family units in general has already been noted.

In Kamachchode the mother-centeredness of the family is particularly marked due to the fact that men are frequently out in the sea fishing. However, there are broad-based structural factors contributing to matrilineal and matrilocal tendencies found in urban low-income communities in many parts of the world [2]. Among the relevant factors are high degree of marital instability in these communities and the resulting increase in the number of female-headed households, the greater mobility of men compared to women, and the role of women in the domestic sphere.

Relative to the larger society, marital instability tends to be much higher in watta communities. The change of marriage partners by both men and women is quite common. Arranged marriages are the exception rather than the rule. Most marriages result from casual love affairs usually with strangers or outsiders. These affairs appear to be an important channel through which outside men get absorbed into these communities. Elopements are rather common and may be seen as a method of circumventing expensive marriage ceremonies. Usually men and women first marry at the age of 20-25 and 18-22 respectively [3].

CASTE

The importance of caste as a principle of watta social organization has been stressed by some previous authors (Kapferer 1977, Karunatilleke 1979). It has been noted that caste affiliations play an important role in the migration process leading to shanty formation. A tendency among certain urban politicians and some business magnates to encourage migration of people from their original home regions has also been noted as a factor contributing to the perpetuation of caste loyalties in the urban setting (Kapferer 1977).

TABLE 4.3

PERCEPTION OF CASTE

Do you expect your son or daughter to choose a marriage partner from within your own caste?	Jude Mawatha		Swarna Mawatha		Soyza Lane		Kamach- chode		Total	
	No.	%	No.	%	No	%	No.	%	No.	%
YES	5	10.2	13	25.5	7	21.2	22	26.5	47	21.7
NO	33	67.3	25	49.0	23	69.7	57	68.7	138	63.9
Not applicable/ No response	11	22.5	13	25.5	3	9.1	4	4.8	31	14.4
Total	49	100,0	51	100.0	33	100.0	83	100.0	216	100.0

There is some evidence that caste affiliations may have played a role in the migration process leading to the formation of some watta communities studied. For instance, as reported earlier, a person known as "Hinna Veda" (the native doctor of Hinna caste), a migrant originating from a coastal town in the South, is said to be a founder of the Jude Mawatha slum community. Similarly those in Soyza Lane in Kandy proudly remember a ruffian called "Hali David", again a migrant from a coastal town in the South, as one of the early heroes of the community. His name as well as place of origin suggest that he belonged to the Salagama caste, which is concentrated in the southern coastal belt of Sri Lanka. Both communities appear to have received a stream of migration from the respective caste groups in the early stage of their development.

While caste may have played some role in the early stages of these communities, none of the contemporary social relations in these communities are determined by caste to any significant extent. The only exceptions are in Swarna Mawatha and Jude Mawatha where there are a few outcast Indian Tamil families engaged in despised occupations such as toilet cleaning. As far as possible, association with the latter is avoided by their neighbors [4].

As evident from Table 4.3, the parents in only 22 percent of the households surveyed expect their children to choose marriage partners from within their own caste groups. This shows that the significance of caste as a determinant of social relations in watta communities studied is quite limited. The perception of caste is highest in Kamachchode, followed by Swarna Mawatha, Soyza Lane and Jude Mawatha. On the whole the perception of caste is higher in shanty communities compared to inner-city slums. This in turn reflects

117

that the carry-over of rural values may be more marked in the former.

ETHNICITY

Ethnicity and ethnic relations among the watta-dwellers deserve special attention in view of the delicate ethnic situation presently prevailing in Sri Lanka. The ethnic composition of the communities studied is given in Table 4.4. Apart from Soyza Lane, all other communities have a sizable number of households belonging to ethnic minorities. Even in Soyza Lane the predominantly Sinhalese Buddhist population have intermingled heavily with the Muslims in some neighboring communities. While the sample communities may not be fully representative of the slum and shanty population at large with regard to ethnic composition, there appears to be a tendency towards over-representation of certain minority groups among the urban poor in all three cities included in the study.

In order to identify any distinctive features in the ethnic composition of the watta communities, we may compare the relative position of each ethnic group in Sri Lanka as a whole, in the Colombo city and in the study communities (see Table 4.4). The Sinhalese representation in these communities is comparable to that in the country as a whole. However, relative to the Colombo city there is a higher proportion of Sinhalese in the study communities. There are much fewer Sri Lanka Tamils in the watta communities studied as compared to Colombo city and Sri Lanka as a whole. While Sri Lanka Tamils account for as much as 22 percent of the Colombo city population, their presence in all four communities studied is only four percent. Thus the findings of the present study suggest that the Sri Lanka Tamils may be considerably under-represented among the urban poor in urban areas outside of the Northern and Eastern provinces [5].

118

TABLE 4.4

PERCENTAGE DISTRIBUTION OF POPULATION ACCORDING TO ETHNICITY:
SRI LANKA, COLOMBO CITY AND STUDY COMMUNITIES

Ethnic Group	1981 Sri Lanka	Colombo City	1983/84 Study Communities					
			JM	SM	SL	KM	Total
Sinhalese	74.0	50.1	79.5	51.0	91.0	71.1	70.2
S.L. Tamil	12.7	22.2	14.5	0	3.0	1.2	4.3
Ind. Tamil	5.5	1.9	2.0	49.0	3.0	0	13.0
Muslim	7.1	23.4	4.0	0	3.0	26.5	12.0
Other	0.8	2.4	0	0	0	1.2	0.5
Total	100.0	100.0	100.0	100.0	100.0	100.0	100.0
N	14,847,000	585,776	302	275	195	554	1,326

S.L. Tamil = Sri Lankan Tamil   Ind. Tamil = Indian Tamil

In contrast, the Indian Tamil population in Colombo and other cities tend to be largely concentrated in selected slum and shanty communities. In addition to certain categories of urban workers of Indian origin present especially in certain inner-city slum areas from the colonial era (for details see Jayawardena 1972), in more recent times certain shanty communities in Colombo appear to have received a considerable inflow of Indian Tamils from the plantation areas. For instance, the bulk of the more recent migrants in Swarna Mawatha, constituting nearly a half of the total population in the community in 1983, were Indian Tamils originating from the plantation areas.

There is a significant Muslim population including Malays in inner-city slums in both Colombo and Kandy [6]. While there is a higher Muslim representation in the study population compared to the country as a whole, relative to their presence in the city population, the Muslims are under-represented in the study communities. In sum, as far as the ethnic composition of the study communities is concerned, while the Sinhalese representation in these communities is proportional to that in Sri lanka as a whole, there is an under-representation of Sri Lanka Tamils and to a lesser extent Muslims.

Other than the ethnic composition per se, it is perhaps more important to consider the nature of ethnic identity and relations among the watta-dwellers. According to some recent theories, the strength of ethnic identity among the members of an ethnic group varies inversely with their class position, i.e. the lower the class position the stronger one's ethnic identity tends to be (Hechter 1978). Thus it is argued that while the black doctors in the US consider themselves doctors first and blacks second, the opposite holds true for the black unemployed. According to this theory, we may expect a stronger ethnic identity among the watta-dwellers compared to higher income groups in each city. The watta-dwellers' active role in recent waves of ethnic violence in cities in turn may be interpreted as facts supporting the above thesis.

This study, however, did not find that the ethnic identities within the communities studied were exceptionally strong. On the contrary, the ethnic identity among the watta-dwellers is rather fluid as manifested in several ways. First, cohabitation between men and women of different ethnic backgrounds tends to be more common in the watta communities compared to the society at large. For instance, in Soyza Lane, where there was a long history of Sinhalese women living with Muslim men, in 1984 there were two cases of interethnic cohabitation, one between a Sinhalese woman and a Muslim man and the other between an Indian Tamil woman and a Sinhalese man. In addition, five cases of interethnic cohabitation were reported in Swarna Mawatha, two in Jude Mawatha and two in Kamachchode. In all these instances a Sinhalese partner lived with a member of minority ethnic group, and their children tended to be identified with the Sinhalese. These interethnic cohabitations, however, signify a relative weakening of ethnic sentiments within these communities.

Second, as Catholicism is the predominant religion among the Sinhalese and some Tamils in a large number of watta communities (e.g. Jude Mawatha and Kamachchode), and since all religions among the watta-dwellers tend to be highly syncretic in character as will be elaborated later, the ethno-religious sentiments like those attached to the Sinhala-Buddhist identity, can be expected to be relatively weak in watta communities. Third, irrespective of their ethnic background many watta-dwellers are bilingual, i.e. able to speak both Sinhala and Tamil. An extreme case is Kamachchode, where the ethnically Sinhalese speak

Tamil as their mother tongue, as typical of fishing communities in the area. In this context it is unlikely that "linguistic nationalism" will appeal strongly to the watta-dwellers. Finally, as will be discussed later, cultural influences like Tamil films are popular among the watta-dwellers in general, irrespective of their ethnic background. These circumstances may be seen as factors inhibiting the growth of strong ethnic consciousnesses among the watta-dwellers.

This is, however, not to say that ethnicity is totally irrelevant for social relations within the wattas. Rather, our position is that the ethnic sentiments among the watta-dwellers should not be overemphasized. In most wattas ethnically different people live side by side in adjoining housing units with considerable unity (see Map 6). With the exception of Kamachchode, where there is a tendency among the Muslims to live close to one another (see Map 10), no pattern of residential segregation within these communities was observed. Apart from the neighborhood ties, the gangs (especially the adult ones) often contained members of different ethnic groups. In Soyza Lane there were some Muslim youths of unknown origin living permanently in some Sinhalese households.

As also noted by some previous studies, there is a pattern of occupational specialization of ethnic groups within each watta community (Marga Institute 1979a, 1979b). In Kamachchode, while the Sinhalese Catholics are engaged in fishing and sale of fish, retail trade in other commodities is mostly in the hands of the Muslims. In Swarna Mawatha, a large number of Indian Tamils serve as domestic servants in nearby high-income households. There are designated Indian Tamil families specializing in toilet cleaning, street sweeping and other such outcast occupations in both Jude Mawatha and Swarna Mawatha. Of the different ethnic groups, the Muslims have benefited most from the employment avenues in the Middle East.

To some degree there may be an unequal relationship between the majority and minority ethnic groups within a watta community. For instance, in Swarna Mawatha most of the Indian Tamils occupy shanty units rented from the original Sinhalese inhabitants in the community headed by Achchi. The latter prefers to rent out her shanty units to Indian Tamils in view of the weaker position and poor housing expectations of the latter. However, her Indian Tamil tenants resent the fact that she abuses them openly for being untidy, especially in regard to their toilet habits. Some of the Indian Tamils in the community also complained that their Sinhalese neighbors abused them frequently after getting drunk. Similarly the two Tamil inhabitants in Soyza Lane complained that when representations were made to the authorities concerning the grievances of the community, the Sinhalese community leaders did not make a sufficiently strong case on their behalf.

Some of the Tamil households in Jude Mawatha and Swarna Mawatha reported that they did not want to mix too much with their Sinhalese neighbors.

As we shall discover in the next chapter, another important factor contributing to the perpetuation of ethnic differences among the watta-dwellers is the segregated ethnic schools that prevail in the vicinity of watta neighborhoods.

Finally, the previously mentioned capacity among the watta-dwellers to resolve conflicts among themselves internally applies to instances of ethnic confrontation within the watta communities as well. Therefore, such instances of friction rarely escalate beyond the inter-household level.

123

THE WATTA-DWELLERS AND THE RIOTS OF JULY 1983

The character of ethnicity in watta communities can be further assessed by examining the nature of their participation in the ethnic violence of July 1983. All four watta communities studied included certain social elements that had directly participated in street violence and looting during this nationwide outbreak of ethnic riots. At the time of fieldwork (late 1983), certain people from these communities were serving prison sentences for offenses committed during July 1983. There were others who had been taken into police custody on suspicion of involvement in the above riots and later released due to lack of evidence against them or pressure from local politicians.

While the urban riots of July 1983 were a part of a nationwide outbreak of ethnic violence, to a considerable extent, they manifested growing contradictions within the urban society. The watta-dwellers, now comprising a bulk of the population in Colombo and other cities, appear to have been in the forefront of these riots. Despite the fact that the ethnic minorities themselves (with the possible exception of Sri Lanka Tamils) are widely present within the wattas, sections of the urban poor made use of this opportunity to attack a segment of the upper classes. To a large extent, the urban riots of July 1983 may be seen as an occasion where the gang activities of the watta-dwellers spread over most cities in Sri Lanka.

Even though it has been pointed out that there was an element of planning, conscious provocation, and even some masterminding behind the 1983 riots (Tambiah 1986), the data from the four communities studied indicate that their participation in these riots was largely spontaneous in character. Given the nature of gang activities in these communities, a tendency towards a general breakdown of law and order in the

124

country was likely to result in a mass mobilization of watta-dwellers almost instantly. Some vicious rumors and a widespread belief among the watta-dwellers that the law enforcement authorities would turn a blind eye towards offenses committed against the Tamils subsequent to the massacre of some 13 Sinhalese soldiers in the North precipitated the riots. The watta gang leaders and their followers took to the streets and attacked Tamil-owned business establishments along the streets and Tamil homes mostly in high-income areas. Looting appears to have been a primary motive of their attacks. The gangs from each watta tended to attack Tamil homes some distances away from their neighborhoods, so that they could not be identified by the victims. The concealed nature of the watta neighborhoods and at the same time their proximity to high-income neighborhoods appear to have facilitated the activities of the looters. During the riots gossip, rumors and information quickly spread among the rioters through the informal communication networks linking various watta communities in each city.

One important but hitherto neglected aspect of these riots was the attitude of the rioters towards their fellow watta-dwellers who were Tamils. The view that during these riots the watta-dwellers turned against themselves along ethnic lines is simply not supported by our data (cf. Kapferer 1988). There were no attacks whatsoever on the Tamil watta-dwellers in any of the four communities studied. On the contrary, the rioters came forward to give protection to the fellow watta-dwellers who were Tamils where the later were under some kind of threat from those in surrounding communities. The riots were unrelated to, and had no effect on any of the inter-ethnic skirmishes that erupted in the watta communities from time to time. During the period of ethnic violence, many outside friends and relatives of the Tamil watta-dwellers came to stay with the latter, using the watta as a place of refuge [7]. In contrast, only one Tamil family in all

125

four communities studied sought outside refuge during the riots.

Another important feature was that the rioters from the watta communities themselves were not ethnically homogeneous. Apart from the Sinhalese, some segments of ethnic minorities, including a few Tamil youths from the wattas, took part in the attack on the rich Tamils. Given the fact that the gangs within the watta communities were often multiethnic in composition, the ethnic heterogeneity among the rioters was not surprising.

Moreover, during the riots there was some degree of class tension expressed independently of ethnic sentiments. For instance, those in Swarna Mawatha made use of this opportunity to threaten one of their enemies, a Sinhalese, in a nearby high-income neighborhood. There were also certain gang leaders in Kamachchode and Soyza Lane who were Sinhalese and who gave protection to some of the Tamil shops in the respective towns, supposedly after receiving protection money from the proprietors concerned.

Contrary to the expectations of the watta-dwellers, following the riots there were numerous police raids on the watta neighborhoods. There was a thorough search for looted goods and where suspected items were found arrests were made. Much to the dismay of the watta-dwellers, the July 1983 riots led to a sharp increase in police vigilance over the wattas.

On the whole the urban riots of July 1983 manifested a considerable overlapping of ethnic and class tensions. On the one hand it reflected the unity among the inhabitants of each watta despite ethnic differences among them; on the other it manifested growing contradictions within the urban society of Sri Lanka.

CLASS

There is some degree of class differentiation within each of the watta communities studied. For instance, one successful entrepreneur in Soyza Lane had multiple business activities including, an ice-cream business, an unauthorized entertainment parlor and money-lending at high interest rates to local vendors. A fair number of other households in the community depended on him for their livelihood. In the other three communities there are important income differences mostly related to new incomes from Middle-East employment [8]. These intra-community income differences, however, cannot be over exaggerated. Even the richest layer of people in a watta broadly share the poor living conditions in their respective neighborhood. Further, there is a marked tendency towards redistribution of wealth within each community. Those who achieve a significant level of upward social mobility normally move out of the watta communities altogether and sever all connections with them. As watta communities in each city are physically scattered and as the work places of the watta-dwellers too are widely distributed, there is hardly any city-wide class solidarity among the watta inhabitants. Of the three cities included in the study, only in Negombo was there any attempt to form a city-wide organization representing all low-income inhabitants of the city (details given below). On the other hand each of the watta communities studied had developed some vertical links with certain urban politicians outside of these communities. The favors of these politicians were sought by the watta-dwellers especially in their dealings with the state and municipal authorities.

FORMAL ORGANIZATIONS

In addition to the informal social organizational principles described so far in this chapter, there are

127

some important formal organizations in some of the watta communities. The Jude Mawatha community has no formal organizations at all. This perhaps reflects the high degree of social disorganization generally found in an inner-city slum. In Swarna Mawatha, in contrast, a Community Development Council (CDC) has been in operation since 1984. This organization is seen by the local inhabitants as a vehicle for obtaining required government assistance for improving latrines, water supply and other facilities in the community. The local CDC has been instrumental in the establishment of two sets of water-sealed latrines and several new water taps in the community. Through an active leader in the community, it is also connected to the local branch of a political party organization affiliated to the ruling government.

In Soyza Lane there had been a succession of organizations from time to time, all seeking to withstand the organized efforts by the KMC to relocate the community. In 1984 an organization called "The Welfare Society of Soyza Lane" had emerged as a vehicle for campaigning against the latest relocation efforts by the Municipality. The organization had formal office-bearers and it raised a community fund of Rs.900 immediately after its formation. A deputation from this organization met several local and national level politicians including the Prime Minister of Sri Lanka at the time and presented the community's arguments against relocation. This organization successfully delayed the actual relocation of the community for a considerable length of time, but in the end the organization became weaker due to disputes among its leaders.

As mentioned earlier, Kamachchode is included in a city-wide organization called the United People's Organization in Negombo (UPON), which has evolved since 1980 as a popular organization representing all slum and shanty inhabitants in the town. A local

Catholic group led by an active priest founded this
organization, having received an inspiration from the
successful re-building of houses gutted by a fire in
one of the local shanty communities through collective
self-help efforts in the community. In 1984 the UPON
had a total membership of about 2,000 families covering virtually all low-income neighborhoods in Negombo.
A person from Kamachchode served as the president of
this organization. While its activities focused mainly
on relieving the housing problem among the urban poor
in Negombo, they also included efforts to organize
poor fishing families, employment generation for
women, credit facilities, promotion of savings,
educational activities catering mainly to school
dropouts in poor urban communities, and some cultural
and recreational programs catering generally to youths
in these communities. The UPON had become an important
mouthpiece for the urban poor in Negombo in their
dealings with the municipality and other relevant
government and non-government organizations. As a
city-wide organization, the UPON had a strong base in
the various low-income communities in the town.
However, the principle of self-help propagated by this
organization was not fully appreciated by many of the
community members. Further, some community members
complained that this organization only benefited a
handful of people connected to its leadership.

SUMMARY AND CONCLUSION

The inhabitants of each watta are bound together
as a community through neighborhood ties, shared
experiences, common interests and, in some instances,
through community-wide formal organizations. Age, sex,
family and kinship and, to a lesser extent, caste,
ethnicity and income differences constitute important
bases of group formation within the watta communities.
The high regard for masculinity and at the same time
the mother-centered nature of the family, the high
rate of female-headed households, the fluidity of

ethnic identities and the role of gangs are among the distinctive features of the watta social organization. On the basis of the strength of kinship ties, presence or absence of active formal organizations, the degree of internal conflict and the rate of deviance, the shanty communities may be said to have higher degree of social organization and control compared to inner-city slums. However, social life in any of the communities studied cannot be described in purely negative terms like marginality, rootlessness and anomie.

The rapid escalation of violence throughout Sri Lanka since 1983 manifested a growing unrest among various underprivileged sections of the Sri Lankan society, including the urban poor. Ironically, such unrest has taken the form of ethnic rather than class hostilities.

NOTES

1. A detailed analysis of the role of football in watta communities is given in Chapter Five.

2. See, for instance, Lewis (1965).

3. However, at present women in particular tend to delay their marriages due to Middle-East employment.

4. There are some low-caste ethnic enclaves in several cities in Sri Lanka. Examples are Mahaiyawa in Kandy and Polkumbura and Kudamakka in Gampola. For details see Silva (1984). There is also some reference to a Rodiya caste shanty community in Colombo city (Karunatilleke 1979:144).

5. A sample survey of 660 slum and shanty households selected randomly from 27 locations in Colombo city gives the following ethnic breakdown: Sinhalese (54%), Tamil (20%), Muslims (25%), others (1%).Unfortunately this study does not distinguish between Sri

130

Lanka Tamils and Indian Tamils. For further information regarding ethnic composition in selected slum and shanty locations see Chapter 4 to 7 in Marga (1979 b). For a discussion on the geographical distribution and the economic role of various ethnic groups in Colombo city see Marga (1979 a).

6. See Ariyaratna (1979) and Fernando (1979).

7. Similarly Ariyaratna (1979) reports of an influx of Muslims from various parts of the country into slum areas in Aluthkade and Masangasvidiya during the 1915 Sinhala-Muslim riots.

8. For details see Chapter Three.

CHAPTER FIVE

POPULAR CULTURE

It is often held that the beliefs, attitudes and the practices of the urban poor do play an important role in perpetuating their poverty. This view is most openly and controversially expressed in the theory of culture of poverty. As formulated by Oscar Lewis (1965), culture of poverty consists of the following pathological attributes.

1. The lack of effective participation and integration of the poor in the major institutions of the larger society, including banks, schools, hospitals and trade unions.

2. Lack of community-level organization beyond nuclear or extended family.

3. Even the institution of family is constantly under threat due to lack of protection during childbirth, early initiation into sex, lack of formalities in entering married life, frequent break-up of families, a trend towards mother-centered families and sibling rivalries.

4. Physical attributes including a sense of despair, marginality, helplessness, dependence and powerlessness.

The first of these attributes will be relevant to the issues discussed in the next two chapters. In the preceding chapter we already considered some aspects of the second and third attributes listed above. The main issue addressed in the present chapter is how far the watta-dwellers are overcome by a sense of despair.

We will begin with a brief consideration of some of the overt symbols, namely language and dress, manifesting what might be called, "the watta subculture". Subsequently we will examine the deeper significance of certain selected aspects of this subculture, namely, a) sports and recreation and b) religion.

LANGUAGE

The language spoken by the watta-dwellers has several distinctive features which are sometimes identified through pejorative terms like "slum language" or "pavement language". While a thorough linguistic analysis of the watta language was beyond the scope of the present study, several peculiarities of their language were noted.

One important finding of this study is that irrespective of their ethnic background, a considerable proportion of the watta inhabitants, especially those in slum communities, are bilingual, i.e., able to speak and understand both Sinhala and Tamil, the two main languages spoken in Sri Lanka. As noted earlier, this may be seen as an aspect of the ethnic heterogeneity and intermixture in watta communities. To some extent, Tamil may be seen as the lingua franca of the watta-dwellers in inner-city areas where there are heavy concentrations of Tamils and Muslims.

Even in Soyza Lane, where a bulk of the people are Sinhalese, certain categories of workers, like natamis and pavement hawkers, are essentially bilingual at work. While a vast majority of the non-Sinhalese in the four study communities do speak Sinhala besides Tamil, which is their mother tongue, many of the

134

Sinhalese watta-dwellers too have acquired at least a smattering of Tamil. In this regard a special circumstance prevails in Kamachchode due to the fact that the Sinhalese in this area traditionally speak Tamil as a home language.

The Sinhalese spoken in these communities has a number of special features. The frequent occurrence of words borrowed from Tamil and English languages is one such feature. Tamil words like "Dorai", "Natami", and "Kachal" and English words like "Robbery", "Scene", and "Bomb" frequently occur in the spoken Sinhalese among the watta-dwellers [1]. These borrowed words, however, are typically used in corrupted forms. Certain English words are invariably used in their plural form.

e.g. 1. Films ekak balanna yanawa.
(We go for a film).

2. Songs ekak ahamuda?
(Shall we listen to a song?).

3. Bombs ekak gahawwa.
(Attacked with a bomb).

The borrowed words may also be recognized by their peculiar accent. For instance, the English word "security" is normally pronounced in watta communities as "sikurity", e.g., "sikurity kenek" (security guard).

Table 5.1 lists some key words occurring largely, though not exclusively, in watta language. These linguistic usages reveal, to some extent, the world view, concerns and even the underworld activities of the watta-dwellers.

135

TABLE 5.1

SOME KEY USAGES IN WATTA LANGUAGE

Word	Literal Meaning	Actual Meaning
Kachal	pandemonium	trouble
Machan	brother-in-law	a term of address used among equals
Dorai	gentleman	a term of address the watta-dwellers use, when talking to rich people
Kepenawa	being cut	victimized/discriminated against
Ussanawa	lift	steal, take away a girl
Suddayak danawa/ Suddakaranawa	to clean	to rob, to pick a pocket
Badu	goods	drugs/illicit liquor
Valiya/ Validanawa Validagnnawa	get entangled	to fight, to get involved in a fight
Jarawakanawa	eat dirt	take bribes
Dappi	bottle top	bomb

Another special feature of the watta dialect is the frequent occurrence of what linguists refer to as "echo compounds", uttered merely for auditory effect.

e.g. 1. "<u>Api nawwalata annasi bannasi deela whisky bisky gannawa</u>."
(We give pineapples to ships and obtain whisky in return).

2. "<u>Car bar natuwata apith minissu tamai</u>."
(We have no cars of our own but we too are people)

Moreover, the watta people tend to be quite boisterous even in friendly day-to-day conversations.

Each watta community use certain code words to refer to objects that are specially significant for those in the community. For instance, in Soyza Lane, where pavement hawking is a primary occupation, a wayside betel stand is simply referred to as a "<u>tattuwa</u>" (lit. tray).

Thus there is a variety of linguistic devices and usages that appear to be peculiar to the watta-dwellers. For someone who is familiar with the watta dialect, it is not difficult to identify a watta-dweller as distinguished from other categories of urban residents simply by listening to his or her speech.

DRESS

The field investigators found some distinctive features in the kind of dress worn by the watta-dwellers. As for the color of their dress both men and women have a distinctive preference for sharp colors. Among the youths in particular there seems to be a preference for silk and nylon as against cotton clothing. The familiar rural dress of cloth and jacket is popular among the older watta women. Inside their homes some of the middle-aged women are seen wearing a one-piece-cloth (i.e. cloth without a jacket) tied under their armpits, a definite sign of their poverty. As reported earlier, exchange of certain items of clothing, like shirts and sarees, is quite common among friends, relatives and neighbors in watta communities.

SPORTS AND RECREATION

The watta-dwellers attach a great deal of importance to sports, music, films and other forms of recreation. Nearly two percent of the average monthly expenditure of households is spent on recreational activities of one kind or another. Contrary to the assumptions implicit in the culture of poverty thesis, the poverty of the watta-dwellers is not necessarily accompanied by a sense of despair and withdrawal from life.

Music is very much a part of the social life in the watta communities. The radios coupled with cassette players (referred to as "two-in-ones") are available in nearly 35 percent of all households in the four communities. The inhabitants especially admire baila (local pop music which had its origins in the Portuguese era) and songs by popular local artists like Desmond Silva, Preddie Silva and Nihal Nelson. In Colombo there are some traveling musicians who go around the watta communities especially in the evenings, entertaining the residents often with improvised musical instruments. The youths from the respective communities often join these musicians in singing and dancing, creating a party-like atmosphere in the whole community. The youths in Soyza Lane have arranged with a nearby Record Bar to play popular songs loudly, so that those in the community can listen to them. At times the young men from the community dance to the rhythms of "hot" music from this nearby music center.

Film-going is a popular form of entertainment among the urban poor in Sri Lanka. While their frequency of film attendance was not examined here, the significance of films for them was apparent in several ways. Often the watta communities are situated in close proximity to cinema halls. For instance, there are as many as five cinema halls situated within easy reach of Swarna Mawatha (see Map 5). In addition to regular cinema halls, there are makeshift entertainment centers showing video films especially appealing to the urban poor in and around many of the watta communities. For instance, one businessman in Soyza Lane has converted part of his house into an entertainment parlor with seating capacity for some 25 people. Popularly known within the community as the "Ramani Theater" [2], this establishment employs several local children to find clients for daily video shows from within the community as well as from among the employees of nearby shops and hotels. Each client pays Rs.5 to view a video film lasting one to two hours.

Irrespective of their ethnic background the watta residents have a distinct preference for Tamil and Hindi films. Both local cinema and video theaters knowingly or unknowingly cater to the specific demand from the urban poor. As far as the watta-dwellers are concerned the desired ingredients of a film are fights, comedy, sex, music, dance and the eventual victory of a person's heroic struggle against social injustice. The best loved movie idols include M.G.Ramachandran (MGR), Rajani Kanth and Kamala Hasan, all of whom are cast in the roles of heroes representing the poor and the underprivileged. The themes of the following films popular in one or the other of the communities studied at the time of the survey have a specific bearing on the situation of the urban poor.

139

1. Kuppai Mettu Rajah (The King of the Slum)
2. Pokkiri Rajah (The Homeless Hero)
3. Guru (a film where karate is used as a weapon against social injustice)

The films popular among the urban poor not only project their images and world view, but also influence their behavior, attitudes and the social values. For a while it was fashionable among the youths in one community to wear long sleeve batik shirts in accordance with what they called "Rajani Style" in keeping with the actor. An old Sinhalese woman in Swarna Mawatha reported that she learned to speak and understand Tamil partly through the many Tamil films she saw throughout her life.

There are also several competitive sports and games popular in the four communities. Football is popular in all four communities studied. The indigenous elle game is popular in Jude Mawatha and Kamachchode, which are situated within the cultural region famous for this baseball-like game.

While the watta-dwellers show a considerable interest in the cricket matches being played in their towns, they rarely play it among themselves, with the exception of the children. Women and children in these communities take part in a number of indoor games, including pancha keliya (a game using sea shells) and olinda keliya (a game using a variety of seeds). Finally, card games are popular among older men in these communities.

As football was found to be the most popular sporting activity among the watta-dwellers in general, we will now consider its specific role in relation to the urban poor.

140

FOOTBALL AS A SPORT AMONG THE URBAN POOR

In addition to interviewing the football players in the study communities, this study examined the organizations and activities of football clubs in the Kandy town so as to understand their social base. There was a considerable number of current and former football players in the four communities studied. The survey of football clubs in Kandy revealed that they are distributed mostly in low-income areas in the city. Each club tends to be identified with and draws its players mostly from one or more low-income neighborhoods in the city. Therefore, it was observed that the football matches give rise to a great deal of enthusiasm in the relevant watta communities. Apart from the players themselves, whole communities participate in the game as supporters of their respective teams. Placing of bets between supporters of rival teams is common. At times fights break out between supporters of rival teams during football matches, and often they develop into temporary "warfare" between the respective communities. Such clashes, however, rarely give rise to permanent enmities.

In Kandy there is a District Football Association, and under it exist various registered football clubs (16 in all), which are distributed mainly in low-income neighborhoods in the town (see Map 11). Each football club has several office bearers and sponsors consisting mainly of prominent local politicians, businessmen and other leading citizens of the town.

Each club has one or more football teams with players drawn mainly (though not exclusively) from the specific low-income neighborhoods represented by the club. For instance, the four leading football clubs in Kandy, namely, Madyama Lanka, Sun Rise, Golden Star and Red Diamond, draw their players mainly from the low-income populations in Katukale, Upper Deiyan-

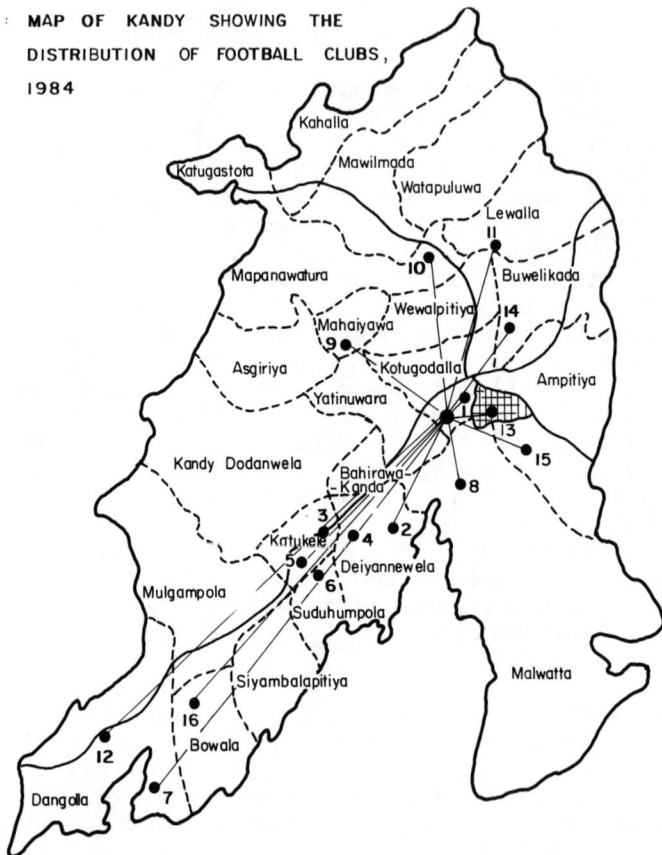

Map II : **MAP OF KANDY SHOWING THE DISTRIBUTION OF FOOTBALL CLUBS, 1984**

No..	Name of Club	Location	No.	Name of Club	Location
1.	Red Diamond	Market	9.	New Mahaiyawa	Mahaiyawa
2.	Sunrise	Upper Deiyannewela	10.	Kennedy	Mapanawatura
3.	Madyarna Lanka	Katukale	11.	Gomas	Lewalla
4.	Golden Stars	Lower Deiyannewela	12.	Lion	Gatambe
5.	Young Olympians	Katukale	13.	King Stars	Colombo Street
6.	Young Wonders	Suduhumpola	14.	Duke of Edinborough	Tannakumbura
7.	Highline	Dangolla	15.	Sisu	Ampitiya
8.	Kandy York	Bogambara	16.	Pubudu	Bowala

newela, Lower Deiyannewela and Central Market respectively. The District Football Association organizes annual football tournaments, for which purpose teams are graded as A, B and C. In addition, there are "gate matches" played at any time of the year with mutual consent of any two football teams. The leading football teams pay their professional players a proportion of income ("gate money") from the matches, but the other teams depend purely on contributions from sponsors, wellwishers and supporters.

In addition to the registered football clubs operating under the District Football Association, there are numerous unregistered football clubs among youths in various low-income neighborhoods. For instance, in Soyza Lane while there is only one star player playing for a recognized football club in Kandy, i.e., Red Diamond, there are two unregistered and unsponsored teams named Mazda (named after a local shop with the same name) and Superstar, consisting of about 20 younger players from the community and from nearby shops. These teams may or may not survive in the years to come, but they serve as springboards from which talented players may leap into recognized football teams in the town.

As a game, football is specially suited and remarkably well-adapted to the circumstances of the urban poor. For the amateurs the cost of playing football is minimal; all they need is a collective investment in a football. The more expensive football gear is used only by the professional players. Especially for unregistered football teams it is difficult to get access to the few playgrounds available in the city. Therefore, the beginners tend to use any open space in the city, including public parks, roads, and building sites, as improvised football fields. With remarkable ingenuity the children from Soyza Lane convert a nearby car park and a market place into temporary football fields in the evening when they play with the help of street lights. Unlike the gentlemen's game of cricket, which is far more time consuming, a football match ordinarily lasts for only one-and-a-half hours, so that the football players and other enthusiasts can make maximum use of the limited time available for leisure after a hard day's work. Like _elle_, unofficial football matches have the capacity to accommodate varying numbers of players, so that play can be started with virtually any number of players who are present. Finally, the spirit of the football game is in keeping with the high social values placed on the display of physical strength, masculinity and competitiveness among the watta-dwellers.

Apart form its entertainment value, the youths in the watta communities tend to consider football as a means of upward social mobility. A common ideal among watta youths is to become leading football stars and through it to achieve social recognition in the town. In a context where opportunities for advancement through education and economic activities are highly restricted, success as football players is seen by these poor urban youths as a more realistic and an attractive goal to achieve. Participation in profes-sional and semi-professional football is also seen as an important qualification for entry into a category of formal sector employment that seems to be open to the urban poor. For instance, a fair number of youths from certain slum and shanty communities in Kandy (Soyza Lane not included) have managed to join the armed forces (typically as soldiers), Prisons Depart-ment (as jailers) or the Postal Department (as postal peons), in part through their success in the football game.

In the Kandy Central Market, which is an important center of the football game in the town, football players appear to be especially welcome as traders, sales assistants or even as load carriers (_natami_).

An important factor is that the football game provides an opportunity for youths from the watta communities to develop contacts with leading citizens of the town, including politicians, who sponsor the game and hold offices in local football clubs. Such contacts are important for the urban poor as a means to influence city administration as well as in several other ways.

The significance of football for slum youths is illustrated by the following example.

Annasi Akman is a seller of pineapples in a prime business location in front of the Central Market. He is 25 years old and he comes from the Soyza Lane slum community. As his business venue is only about 150 meters away from Soyza Lane, he can successfully run a lucrative pineapple business in a central location where trading is prohibited under Municipal By-Laws. Akman is married and has two children aged four and two. He is a frontline football player in the Red Diamond Football Club, of which he is a founder member. In the bazaar he has established himself as a robust man who is respected to some extent even by the police.

Like many others in Soyza Lane, Akman was brought up in a single-parent household, having had no known father. His mother, who was a well-known betel seller in the town has had many short term affairs with men but none resulting in a marriage. Akman dropped out of Punyasampadaka Vidyalaya [3] after reaching Grade Five. As a teenager he began life as a _natami_ at the Central Bus Stand. Later he was employed by a local pineapple vendor as an itinerant seller of pineapple pieces. Then he became a stationary vendor selling (whole) pineapples to passing customers in partnership with a Muslim businessman.

At present, Akman is a leading pineapple trader in the town, his daily profits from the business averag-

145

ing about Rs.200 (U.S. $ 6.70 as at 1984). He has three helpers working under him. He has also acquired a market stall in a nearby market place which has been temporarily leased to another businessman known to him. While his economic achievements up to now cannot be exaggerated, he has certainly achieved a degree of upward social mobility over the years.

To Akman, the progress he has made as a football player so far is much more significant than any of his business achievements. As a leading football player in the Red Diamond Football Club he considers himself a professional. His football talents are widely recognized throughout the city.

As he recalls, he started off his football career as a child; he played with other children in Soyza Lane whenever they had the time and opportunity. After he joined the pineapple business, he and several others involved in the pineapple trade near the Central Market began to play football in a somewhat more organized fashion using a car park near the market as their regular playground in the evenings. The football team that evolved there became appropriately known as "Annasi Bullets" (lit. Pineapple Bullets). Those involved in Annasi Bullets later formed the Red Diamond Football Club, which subsequently became a registered club under the District Football Association. By 1984 the Red Diamond Football Club, though it still ranked as a B grade team, had become a frontline football team in the town.

Akman's life has considerably changed due to his commitment to football. In order to maintain his health and physical strength, Akman completely refrains from smoking and alcohol consumption, vices which are deeply entrenched in Soyza Lane. He has also been a leading advocate of social and moral reform within the Soyza Lane community. He is determined to give a good education to his children, and his elder

146

daughter has been admitted to the YMCA preschool, one of the two children from Soyza Lane privileged to receive preschool education. One of his patrons in the Red Diamond Football Club helped him to admit his daughter to this preschool.

The foregoing analysis shows that the urban poor are not necessarily entrapped in a culture of poverty. Their passionate involvement in football demonstrates that, instead of permanently and fatalistically accepting their state of poverty, the watta-dwellers clearly look for every possible avenue of advancement open to them and make the maximum use of available urban space and the limited time available for their recreation. On the whole, their involvement in sports should be encouraged as an aspect of their positive adaptation to the goals of the larger society.

So far we examined certain aspects of popular culture among the watta-dwellers. We will next consider the nature of their religious beliefs and practices.

RELIGION

There is a complex pattern of religious beliefs and practices in each watta community. As seen in Table 5.2, each of the major religions in the country are represented within the four study communities.

As compared to Sri Lanka and Colombo city as a whole, there is a notable under-representation of Buddhists and a substantial over-representation of Catholics in the study communities. While admitting that our sample may be considerably biased in respect of religious composition due to the inclusion of two predominantly Catholic communities (i.e. Jude Mawatha in Colombo and Kamachchode in Negombo), it is nevertheless true that a significant part of the western coastal belt, where there is a heavy concentration of

147

TABLE 5.2

PERCENTAGE DISTRIBUTION OF POPULATION ACCORDING TO RELIGION:
SRI LANKA, COLOMBO AND THE STUDY COMMUNITIES

Religion	Sri Lanka 1981	Colombo 1981	Study Communities (1883/84)				
			JM	SM	SL	KM	All
Buddhist	69.3	43.0	34.1	49.5	91.0	2.4	34.1
Hindu	15.5	16.8	9.8	31.6	6.0	1.2	11.1
Muslim	7.6	24.3	4.9	0	3.0	27.7	12.5
Catholic	6.8	12.9	48.8	13.4	0	68.7	40.4
Christian	0.7	2.5	2.4	5.5	0	0	1.9
Other	0.1	0.6	0	0	0	0	0
Total	100.0	100.0	100.0	100.0	100.0	100.0	100.0
N	14,847,000	585,776	302	275	195	554	1,326

the urban poor, is predominantly Catholic. Certain new trends in the Catholic Church in Sri Lanka, including increased radicalization of some segments of the church, in turn, can be seen as a response to the predominance of the urban poor among the Catholic population in contemporary Sri Lanka. Parallel changes, however, may be occurring in other religions in Sri Lanka too in response to specific socio-religious needs of the poor.

Even though the watta-dwellers identify themselves as Buddhists, Catholics and so on, the religion practiced by them is in many ways a syncretic one. Buddhists seeking the blessings of Hindu or Catholic shrines and vice versa are quite common. Irrespective of their religious denominations, almost all households in a community participate in the major religious festivals celebrated there, such as the celebration of the patron saints in Kamachchode, and the Wesak celebrations in Swarna Mawatha. Similarly, many of the Buddhist youths in Jude Mawatha join their Catholic friends in the annual pilgrimage to the Catholic shrine of Thalawila. In a tragic accident a Hindu boy in Swarna Mawatha sustained severe spinal injuries when he fell off a tree while picking flowers to be used in a Wesak celebration in the community.

Religious beliefs too have a syncretic character. For instance, according to local beliefs, the patron saint of the Wella Vidiya Church near Kamachchode, i.e., St. Sebastian, originated as a Hindu god, a belief that is in keeping with the fact that the local Sinhalese are Tamil speaking. In Kamachchode there is a St. Sebastian Alms Giving Society (Santa Sebastian Dana Samithiya), which provides alms to the destitute in the city on St. Sebastian day as well as on Wesak day. Many of the beliefs and practices relating to spirit possession, sorcery, charms, astrology etc. are held in common by those of different religious denominations (Kapferer 1983).

149

The problems of the urban poor figure in one way or another within each of the major religions in Sri Lanka. As for the Catholic response, a good example is the Meegamu Eksath Janatha Sangamaya, or UPON, in Negombo, to which reference was made earlier. Beyond the conventional Catholic approach to relieving poverty by means of charity and relief work, this organization seeks to promote collective action among the urban poor in the whole city in order to overcome their common problems. The church itself, while providing various facilities to this organization, remains in the background. The organization actively seeks the support of the local leadership of other religions as well. Another Catholic group active in both Jude Mawatha and Kamachchode was called "Pubuduwa" (Renewal). Among other things it stressed the importance of plainness and simplicity in dress, consumption, etc.

While we did not come across any concerted effort within the Islamic establishment to address urban poverty as far as the study communities were concerned, a religious custom known as "sadaka" appeared to be somewhat important in redistributing a part of the profits made by the rich Muslims. Under this custom Muslims in Kamachchode received some charity from the Muslim businessmen in the town, especially during the Ramazan period. Among the Muslims in a nearby shanty community a new Islamic cult called "The Hadiniya Cult" had posed a considerable challenge to the orthodox Islamic faith. This new cult contained several elements borrowed from Catholicism, the predominant religion in the area. Its significance for the urban poor, however, was not explored in this study.

The complex relationship between the Buddhist institutions and the urban poor was evident in Kandy. While the traditional monastic establishment in Kandy

150

consisting of temples belonging to the Siamese Fraternity (Siam Nikaya) remained somewhat aloof vis-a-vis the watta-dwellers, certain newly established Buddhist temples, mainly affiliated with the Amarapura Nikaya, catered to the social and religious needs of this important urban group. The priests in local Siam Nikaya temples had refused to visit Soyza Lane for funeral services or for any other religious observances, ostensibly because of the community's association with crime, prostitution and other vices. Moreover, in certain other areas in Kandy there was a direct confrontation between the Siam Nikaya temples and the local shanty-dwellers due to the fact that the latter were illegally occupying temple lands.

Against the above background the lay Buddhists in slum and shanty communities in Kandy have largely turned to several newly-emerged Amarapura Nikaya temples for their religious requirements. In fact the emergence of these new Buddhist temples in Kandy may have been associated with the expansion of the low-income population in the city. The Bahirawakanda Sri Mahabodhi Viharaya is a good example of a Buddhist temple in the above category.

Sri Mahabodhi Viharaya of Bahirawakanda is situated at the top of a hill on a picturesque site overlooking the Kandy town (see Map 7). The chief incumbent of the temple, Rev. Dammarama, gradually built up this temple since 1974. Initially the temple was in a mud hut that had been illegally built in a state-owned forest reserve. This evoked considerable opposition from the authorities. Further, as this was an Amarapura Nikaya temple, it also evoked much opposition from the Kandyan monastic establishment. However, Rev. Dammarama was able to withstand this opposition in part due to the patronage he received from several local politicians and also due to the support and encouragement given by certain low-income neighborhoods in the city. Through the vigorous efforts of Rev. Dammarama the temple managed to acquire title to some three acres of land within the forest reserve. Subsequently three new buildings and a parapet wall protecting the much-venerated Bodhi tree on the temple premises were constructed with support and contributions from the lay devotees. In 1984 the temple was still expanding with electricity newly connected and water specially supplied to the temple through Municipal trucks. There were five Buddhist monks and ten disciples staying in the temple. It had plans to construct a 65-foot tall Buddha statue that would be visible to the city center.

The temple had many connections with low-income communities in adjacent areas. According to the chief incumbent, nearly 80 percent of its devotees come from these low-income neighborhoods. The residents of Soyza Lane are among its strongest supporters. They invariably secure the services of this temple in funerals as well as in other household and community functions. Further, this community regards Rev. Dammarama as one of its principal benefactors. The community collectively provides alms to the temple once a month. Several people from Soyza Lane are actively involved in raising funds for the temple, as well as in periodic Bodhi Pujas [4] held in the temple. Aside from the Bodhi Pujas the services of the temple include free public services like Pirith chanting and a variety of other specialized functions like fortune telling, charms, magic and healing which are all done for a fee by the chief incumbent himself.

In the early stage of the temple its lay devotees from the nearby low-income communities signed a petition requesting the authorities to grant permanent land rights to the temple. The residents of Soyza Lane in turn sought the opinion and advice of Rev. Dammarama whenever they were ordered to move out by the authorities. Before 1977 several youths from another slum community in Kandy secured jobs in the Police, Army and the Prison's Department with the help of Rev. Dammarama who in turn used his connections with some local politicians for this purpose. Thus the Bahirawakanda Temple, like its Catholic counterpart in Negombo, performs several socio-cultural and economic functions, as well as religious ones, vis-a-vis its lay devotees from the local watta communities.

SUMMARY AND CONCLUSION

In this chapter we identified several aspects of the watta subculture, including the nature of their dialect, dress, specific tastes as regards music and films, sporting activities and religious cults. We found that in many of these aspects there is a considerable amount of creativity and adaptability on the part of the urban poor. Contrary to the assumptions in the culture of poverty thesis, at least some of the watta-dwellers are upwardly mobile in their orientation.

The point made in the previous chapter about the mixed and heterogenous character of watta society is also applicable to watta culture. The Sinhala-Tamil bilingualism of the watta-dwellers, the widespread popularity of Hindi and Tamil films among all ethnic groups, and their religious syncretism can be seen as aspects of a composite and considerably open subculture.

Watta-dwellers may be best approached for various developmental purposes using their own dialect and the kind of media (music, films etc.) best liked by them. This appears to be the essence of the Jana Udawa Sannivedana Program (Communication Program for Reawakening the Public) sponsored by the CBA. The effects of this program up to now must be carefully assessed, and efforts must be made to strengthen it further where necessary. Finally, steps must be taken to promote sports and recreational facilities relevant and accessible to the watta-dwellers.

NOTES

1. These borrowed words may occur in spoken Sinhalese in general but among the watta-dwellers they tend to occur more frequently.

2. This name is derived from that of the owner's wife.

3. Described in Chapter Six.

4. Bodhi Pujas center around veneration of sacred Bo trees by decorating them and offering flowers, milk, milk rice etc. to deities believed to inhabit these trees. Bodhi Pujas are often held with the aim of securing the blessings of the relevant deities for success in examinations, employment, business and other such secular activities.

CHAPTER SIX

LITERACY AND EDUCATION

Even though Sri Lanka has evolved a system of free education since the 1940s, so far it has only marginally benefited the urban poor. Pervious research notes the poor educational achievement of slum children and attributes it largely to the negative attitude towards education generated by their home and community environment (Jayasooriya 1955, Manatunga 1982). The nature of educational facilities serving watta neighborhoods per se has received less attention. Hence this study examined both the character of the so-called "watta schools" and how it related to the level of educational achievement of the watta-dwellers. The interaction between the watta schools and their social environment was also examined.

LITERACY

Table 6.1 presents data on adult literacy in the study communities.

Determined according to their self-declared ability to read and understand a Sinhala or a Tamil newspaper, the level of literacy among both male and female heads of households in these communities is rather low compared to national figures. Overall literacy rates for male and female household heads are 64 and 60 respectively as compared with 1981 national literacy rates of 86 and 71 for all males and females respectively. Except for Swarna Mawatha, where females are much less literate compared to males, the

155

TABLE 6.1

PERCENTAGE DISTRIBUTION OF MALE AND FEMALE HEADS OF HOUSEHOLDS
ACCORDING TO LITERACY

Able to read & understand a newspaper?	Jude Mawatha	Swarna Mawatha	Soyza Lane	Kamach- chode	Total
Yes					
Male Head	63.3	74.5	54.5	62.6	64.4
Female Head	57.1	60.8	57.5	62.6	60.2
No					
Male Head	20.4	13.7	18.2	22.9	19.4
Female Head	22.4	35.3	36.5	31.3	30.0
NA/No response					
Male Head	16.3	11.8	27.3	14.5	16.2
Female Head	20.4	3.9	6.0	6.0	9.8
Total					
Male Head	100.0	100.0	100.0	100.0	100.0
Female Head	100.0	100.0	100.0	100.0	100.0
Sample Size	49	51	33	83	216

* The oldest male and female in each household are treated as
  respective household heads for the purpose of this table.

difference between male and female heads of household
in regard to literacy is more or less insignificant in
all other communities. Soyza Lane has the lowest
literacy rate for male heads of household and the
second lowest for female heads of household; this
finding is in agreement with several other measures of
educational achievement to be discussed in the other
sections.

EDUCATIONAL ACHIEVEMENT

In order to understand the level of educational
achievement in the study communities we may consider
how many people in each community have obtained some
selected educational qualifications (see Table 6.2).

TABLE 6.2

NUMBER OF WATTA-DWELLERS WITH SELECTED EDUCATIONAL
QUALIFICATIONS

Highest Qualification	Number of Persons				
	JM	SM	SL	KM	Total
Degree	0	0	0	0	0
GCE-AL	1	0	0	0	1
GCE-OL	4	6	0	9	19
Diploma etc.	2	0	0	1	3
Total	7	6	0	10	23
Above as a % of Adult Population	3.2	3.4	0	3.0	2.8

Thus not a single university graduate is present
in the watta communities studied [1]. That the watta-
dwellers are generally excluded from higher education
is also evident from the fact that only one person

with General Certificate of Education, Advanced Level
(GCE-AL) qualification is present in all four communities. There are three persons with diplomas or
professional qualifications and two of them have
achieved the respective qualifications through their
employment. There are several General Certificate of
Education, Ordinary Level (GCE-OL) qualified persons
in three of the communities. The Soyza Lane community
has a notable absence of any educationally qualified
persons at all.

DROPOUT RATE

The level of educational achievement in the study
communities can be further assessed by examining how
many of the children in the compulsory school-going
ages (6-14) actually attend school. The relevant data
are presented in Table 6.3.

When all four communities are taken together the
dropout rate for children in compulsory school-going
ages is 14 percent. This compares favorably with the
national dropout rate of 16 percent for 1981. Thus the
primary school attendance among watta children appears
to be satisfactory. The highest dropout rate is in the
inner-city slum of Jude Mawatha, followed by Swarna
Mawatha, Soyza Lane and Kamachchode.

As for male-female differences in school attendance, on the whole the dropout rate for boys is 16
percent as against 13 percent for girls. However,
there is considerable variation among study communities as regards male-female differences in school
attendance. Compared to boys, girls have a higher
dropout rate in Swarna Mawatha and, to a lesser
extent, in Jude Mawatha. The pattern is reversed in
Kamachchode and Soyza Lane. In Kamachchode the dropout
rate for boys is substantially higher than that for
girls. The reasons for inter-community differences in
school attendance are not clear. But it is possible

that the labor requirements of the fishing industry
have something to do with the lower male school
attendance in Kamachchode.

TABLE 6.3

SCHOOL DROPOUT RATE IN STUDY COMMUNITIES

	JM	SM	SL	KM	Total
Number of children in 6-14 age group					
Male	37	33	26	77	173
Female	25	31	33	78	167
Total	62	64	59	155	340
Children aged 6-14 not attending school					
Male	6	4	4	14	28
Female	5	6	4	6	21
Total	11	10	8	20	49
Dropout Rate (%)					
Male	16.2	12.1	15.4	18.2	16.2
Female	20.0	19.4	12.1	7.7	12.6
Total	17.7	15.6	13.6	12.9	14.4

Thus while the current level of primary school
attendance among watta children may be satisfactory,
in terms of both adult literacy and the level of
educational achievement, the watta communities have a
rather poor record. We may now consider the extent to
which this poor record may be attributed to any
imbalances in the educational system. We will examine
this by looking at the specific nature of the schools
serving each of the watta communities covered by the
study.

JUDE MAWATHA

The Jude Mawatha slum community is mainly served by three poorly-equipped schools situated within a radius of one kilometer from the community. The names of these schools are Sri Medhananda Buddhist Vidyalaya, St. James' Catholic School and Hamsa Muslim School. As the names indicate the schools serving the area tend to be differentiated on the basis of religion and ethnicity. The conditions in each school are discussed below.

Sri Medhananda Vidyalaya

This school is located within a predominantly slum area. It was started in 1957 within the premises of a Buddhist temple by a group of local philanthropists. Initially the school encountered stiff opposition from some slum landlords, who feared that the school would interfere with their property. As of 1984 it was a mixed school with classes up to grade 10. The total student enrollment was 480 and the teaching staff consisted of 20 members, giving a staff-student ratio of 1 to 24.

As for its physical conditions, the school consisted of three rundown buildings, two of which were two-storied ones, all huddled together in a land area of about 900 square meters. The school had neither a playground nor any other open space to be used for sports and physical training. Much like in the surrounding wattas, crowded and dilapidated conditions prevailed in this school.

When we look at the number of children in each grade we can see a tendency towards a decline in enrollments from grade six onwards (see Table 6.4). Although there are a lesser number of girls in the total enrollment there appears to be a sharp decline in the number of boys enrolled in the highest grades.

160

TABLE 6.4

SRI MEDHANANDA VIDYALAYA: ENROLLMENT BY SEX
AND GRADE, 1984

Grade	Boys	Girls	Total
Preliminary	42	20	62
Grade 1	20	19	39
2	35	28	63
3	10	14	24
4	37	27	64
5	34	26	60
6	24	24	48
7	26	13	39
8	26	14	40
9	7	10	17
10	13	11	24
Total	274	206	480

St. James' School

Prior to the nationalization of schools, this
Catholic primary school was affiliated to a local
church with the same name. According to the longest
serving teacher in the school, this school was
established in 1802 as a missionary school catering to
children from poor fishing families. In more recent
times it has turned into a school serving the local
slum communities. Having classes up to grade five
only, the school had hardly made any progress over a
period of 182 years.

As of 1984 there was a total of 20 teachers
serving some 421 children enrolled in the school. This
gives a staff-student ratio of 1 to 31 for this
school. The entire school premises was about 300

161

square meters in extent. The school buildings consisted of a single story building dating back to the
missionary period and a two-storied building constructed in 1970 subsequent to the government takeover
of the schools.

TABLE 6.5

ST. JAMES' SCHOOL: ENROLLMENT BY SEX AND GRADE, 1984

Grade	Boys	Girls	Total
Preliminary	37	30	67
Grade 1	42	26	68
2	34	31	65
3	40	34	74
4	29	36	65
5	52	30	82
Total	234	187	421

Facilities in the school were far from satisfactory. The roof of the older building was leaking in
many places. There was a number of water taps
installed within the school premises but at the time
of our visit to the school none of them was working.
As in the previous school, St. James' School had no
playground at all. When required children from this
school were taken to a playground in a nearby better
equipped school serving higher income groups.

In 1984 St. James' School had an adequate and
well-qualified staff. However, none of the staff
members came from or had any connection with the local
slum communities served by the school. In recent years
there had been a rapid turnover of staff including the
principals. The only organization which had shown any
long-term interest in the school was the local church

situated next to the school. Its ability to influence the school administration, however, had declined substantially following the government takeover of the school.

As evident in Table 6.5, in this school too there is a higher enrollment of boys. The number in each grade is more or less similar indicating a relative continuity in primary education among those enrolled in this school. However, as of 1984 the school was not officially linked with any secondary school in the area and this meant that for those who completed primary education in St. James' School, some special parental effort was necessary for transferring them to a local secondary school. In the old days children from the local fishing families hardly wished to continue their education beyond St. James' School. Now there may be a greater interest among local children to proceed to secondary education, but the school system operating in the area did not facilitate their smooth transfer to secondary education.

Hamsa Muslim School

Started by a Muslim educator in 1917 and initially affiliated to a nearby mosque, this school now serves the Muslim population in the local slum communities.

In 1984 the school had classes up to grade 10 and a total enrollment of 807 served by 20 teachers. The staff-student ratio of 1 to 40 was quite unsatisfactory. This school, however, was much less crowded compared to the previously mentioned schools. The school had a total land area of about 200 square meters and consisted of five buildings, including one which was under construction.

After 1970 the number of buildings in the school increased from one to five primarily due to special nationwide efforts to improve educational facilities

163

for the Muslims during the 1970s. However, the school had no playground and the staff complained about the lack of amenities, such as rest rooms and toilet facilities. In addition to Muslim children, there were some 16 Tamil children attending this school.

TABLE 6.6

HAMSA MUSLIM SCHOOL: ENROLLMENT BY SEX AND GRADE, 1984

Grade	Boys	Girls	Total
Preliminary	34	29	63
Grade 1	39	27	66
2	33	31	64
3	53	38	91
4	38	40	78
5	92	79	171
6	64	52	116
7	43	36	79
8	20	17	37
9	25	6	31
10	8	3	11
Total	449	358	807

While there is an upward tendency in enrollments up to grade six, the numbers drop sharply thereafter. Although this is a mixed school the total number of girls enrolled is much less than that of boys. When we compare the number of boys and girls in each grade, the boys outnumber the girls in each grade except in grade four. The number of girls in grade nine and ten are exceptionally low both in absolute and relative terms. This reflects the general tendency among the Muslims to discourage the education of girls especially after they attain puberty.

As in the previous schools, this school was not directly linked to any higher school in the city so as to facilitate an easy transfer of its students to senior secondary education. On the whole the schools serving the Jude Mawatha slum community are rather congested and geared to ethnically-specific primary education. They have poor links with the rest of the education system leading to secondary and higher education. While there may have been a few instances of upward social mobility via these schools, on the whole they do not contribute much towards changing the pattern of life in the slum community.

SWARNA MAWATHA

There are some eight schools in the vicinity of Swarna Mawatha. They include well-equipped middle-class schools, such as Isipathana and Lumbini Colleges. While a handful of children from the community have managed to gain admission to these well-to-do schools, a vast majority of the watta children attend three poorly-known local schools with minimum facilities. As described below, two of these schools exclusively serve the many shanty communities in the area.

Lanka Sabha Vidyalaya

This is typical of the schools serving watta neighborhoods. Access to the school is through several shanty communities. Congestion and limitation of space are immediately visible when one steps into the school premises. The children dressed in an untidy manner are seen chatting and loitering in and out of the school premises during much of the school hours. The language of the children and, to some extent, even the language spoken by the teachers indicate a heavy influx of watta language into the school.

165

TABLE 6.7

LANKA SABHA VIDYALAYA: ENROLLMENT BY SEX
AND GRADE, 1984

Grade	Boys	Girls	Total
Preliminary	33	32	65
Grade 1	32	25	57
2	35	17	52
3	12	10	22
4	22	15	37
5	12	18	30
6	15	11	26
7	15	11	26
8	13	7	20
Total	189	146	335

Lanka Sabha Vidyalaya was started in the late 19th century as a missionary school sponsored by a local philanthropist. From the start the school had been meant for children from poor families in the area. The school has had a precarious existence up to its takeover by the government in 1961. Desks and chairs were constantly stolen from the school and the school premises were used by the local thugs as a rendezvous and a venue for various anti-social activities. The school has made some progress since 1980 under the leadership of a dedicated lady principal.

Lanka Sabha Vidyalaya is a mixed primary school with classes up to grade eight. In 1984 there were 335 children on the school register consisting of 252 Sinhalese, 46 Tamil and 37 Muslim children [2]. The teaching staff consisted of 12 trained teachers, two graduates and two teachers with no professional

166

qualifications. This gives a staff-student ratio of 1 to 21. The school comprises one three-storied building with a total floor area of about 900 square meters. The total extent of the school premises is 455 square meters. This school has neither a playground nor any other facilities for sports. According to the principal, congestion within the school and the lack of recreational facilities contributed to the poor discipline among the school children. Even basic facilities such as latrines and water taps are lacking. The school does not charge any facilities fees from the children in view of the poor economic background of their parents. From time to time the school children receive free books and clothing from a number of welfare organizations contacted by the principal.

This school too shows a more or less consistent drop in student numbers in each successive grade. Once again there is a lower enrollment of girls compared to boys. There is a marked drop in enrollment after grade three, especially among girls. This school too did not perceive itself as a primary institution preparing students for any specific higher-level school in the area.

Arethusa Vidyalaya

Situated about one kilometer away from Swarna Mawatha, this school was first started by the Dutch Reformed Church for children from poor Burgher families. At first its medium of instruction was English. The school was converted to a bilingual school during the 1950s and to an exclusively Sinhala medium school during the 1960s. The school has undergone many changes over time, including a change of its venue. As of 1984 the children attending this school came from a variety of backgrounds, including the local shanty communities.

167

TABLE   6.8

ARETHUSA VIDYALAYA: ENROLLMENT BY GRADE, 1984

Grade	Total
Preliminary	59
Grade 1	45
2	57
3	60
4	67
5	65
6	66
7	64
8	55
9	43
10	31
Total	612

Arethusa Vidyalaya is a boys' school with classes up to grade 10. In 1984 the school had a total of 612 children, comprising 398 Sinhalese, 177 Muslims, 23 Tamils and 14 children of unknown ethnicity (probably Burgher children). There were 26 persons serving on the teaching staff, giving a staff-student ratio 1 to 24. The school yard was about 0.8 hectares in extent. There were seven buildings, some of which were over 50 years old. This school had electricity, a science laboratory, a library, a playground and other such facilities typically not available in schools in the sample.

This school does not show a pattern of sharp decline in enrollment in terminal grades. As a qualitatively better school also open to children from middle-income families, only a limited number of shanty children from the area managed to get admission to this school.

Pamankada Tamil School

This school provides education to Tamil-speaking children from several slum and shanty communities in the area, including Swarna Mawatha. Formerly the school was housed in a temporary building some distance away from its present location. Since 1983 the school has been housed in a newly-constructed three-storied building with a floor area of about 667 square meters.

TABLE 6.9

PAMANKADA TAMIL SCHOOL: ENROLLMENT BY SEX
AND GRADE, 1984

Grade	Boys	Girls	Total
1	24	18	42
2	17	22	39
3	26	13	39
4	29	30	59
5	33	23	56
6	31	18	49
7	23	14	37
8	16	12	28
9	16	9	25
10	19	15	34
Total	234	174	408

The total number of boys and girls in classes up to grade 10 were 408, consisting of 350 Tamil and 58 Muslim children. The school suffered heavily due to the ethnic violence of July 1983. Between July 1983 and February 1984 the number of teachers serving in the schools dropped from 21 to 10 because of displacements and transfers. As of 1984 the school had a most unsatisfactory staff-student ratio of 1 to 41 and was without some of the basic amenities and equipment.

As evident from Table 6.9, the school conforms to the standard low-income pattern of lower enrollment for girls. The acting principal of the school noted that both the reduction in staff and the poor school attendance of children following the events of July 1983 were major problems affecting the school. However, the enrollment figures are relatively consistent for all grades, showing a considerable continuity in education within the school.

Thus, with the exception of Arethusa Vidyalaya, the schools serving Swarna Mawatha belong to the standard low-income type. Even though there are a number of well-established schools in the vicinity of Swarna Mawatha, for the most part the watta children are excluded from them. While the enrollment in each school tends to be ethnically-mixed to a greater extent than in Jude Mawatha, the schools in the area are clearly differentiated on the basis of medium of instruction.

SOYZA LANE

Marked inequalities in the education system are manifested in secondary cities as well as in Colombo. Even through certain prominent colleges in Kandy are situated within a short distance from Soyza Lane, this slum community is by and large served by two neglected primary schools situated within the central business area of the city. A brief account of these two schools follows.

170

Kappitipola Vidyalaya

Situated at the back of several business houses facing the Dalada Vidiya and surrounded in other directions by pavement shops, a central bus stand and a garage, this school has a most uncongenial environment. It serves several inner-city slum communities, including Soyza Lane, Deiyannewela and Atupattiya. This school was started by the Baptist Mission in the 1930s and was formerly occupying a prime business location at Dalada Vidiya. Later the school was shifted to its present location as its former premises were gradually acquired by private business establishments.

This is a mixed school with classes up to grade 10. The total number of boys and girls on register is 438. There are 21 teachers in all resulting in a staff-student ratio of 1 to 21. The school consists of a neglected older building and a recently constructed two-storied building. The school premises, which is about 300 square meters in extent, has a prison-like atmosphere due to lack of any open space and the enclosed nature of the school buildings. There is litter thrown in mostly by surrounding business houses all over the school yard. The school buildings are highly overcrowded; in many instances the class rooms are partitioned using cupboards. Having no separate office room, the principal sits in a corner of a building with his office area enclosed by a few cupboards. As one walks through the school one is constantly reminded of physical conditions prevailing in a slum neighborhood.

The staff, which was by and large well qualified, resented being posted in this school. One teacher was of the opinion that his transfer to this school from another one in Kandy was an act of political victimization. The attendance in the school was generally poor. The principal remarked that many children keep

171

away from the school in order to do various odd jobs, such as selling of sweepstakes especially when there are certain festivals in the city.

Punyasampadaka Vidyalaya

This school began in the 1920s as a Buddhist denominational school. It is situated on Yatinuwara Street, some 100 meters away from Soyza Lane (see Map 7). The school is disreputably known as "Ali Muddukkuwa College" showing its identification with the slum community. It is a boy's school with classes up to grade 10. The total number of teachers and students in the school in 1984 were 16 and 246 respectively, giving a staff-student ratio of 1:15. The school consists of a single two-storied building with a total floor area of about 275 square meters. Due to the limitation of space, the school is held in two sessions. As the school is facing a busy street, the classes are constantly disturbed by passing traffic, vendors etc.

The school occupies a prime business location. The principal was of the view that the future of the school was uncertain as some local businessmen and politicians had plans to take over the building for certain other purposes. The staff also commented on the poor discipline among children. Apart from their social background, limitation of space, lack of recreational facilities within the school and various distractions in the school neighborhood were seen as factors contributing to the misbehavior of the children. In the past there had been instances where the parents from nearby slum communities came to the school and abused the teachers for punishing the children on disciplinary matters. There had also been reports of a ring of local prostitutes using the school premises at night with the connivance of the night watchman of the school.

172

Parents in Soyza Lane were fully aware of the limitations of these two schools. They said that they are compelled to send their children to these two schools as they are not accepted by any of the better schools in Kandy. Apart from the high admission fees required by the latter schools, they seem to have certain other mechanisms whereby slum children are excluded. One mother complained "The moment they see our Soyza Lane address, they simply say there are no vacancies in their schools". In a few instances where the children from Soyza Lane did manage to get admission to nearby better school, they were compelled to leave these schools shortly due to the social pressure from the other children there.

KAMACHCHODE

There is a total of six schools within a radius of about two kilometers from Kamachchode. Two of these schools, i.e., St. Mary's Boy's College and Newstead College, largely cater to the high-income group in Negombo. The other four schools cater to several poor neighborhoods, including Kamachchode. Information relating to all six schools are summarized in Table 6.10.

Thus according to the income groups served by them, there is a fine gradation of schools in Negombo. While the schools serving the rich have classes up to university-entrance level (grade 12), the schools catering to the low-income groups are by and large restricted to primary education. Further, it can be seen that while the enrollments in the affluent schools tend to be ethnically mixed, the schools catering to the poor are clearly differentiated on the basis of religion and ethnicity. This has significant implications for both the quality of education in these schools and their impact on social life in the watta communities. There is also significant variation

173

TABLE 6.10

INFORMATION ABOUT SELECTED SCHOOLS IN NEGOMBO, 1984

Name of School	Social Class Served	Highest Grade	No. of Students	No. of Teachers	Staff-Student Ratio	Ethnic Background
St. Mary's Boy's	Upper	12	1,500	55	27.3	Mixed
Newstead Mixed	Upper	12	2,300	80	28.8	Mixed
St. Mary's Mixed	Middle	10	904	27	33.5	S
Kamachchode Muslim	Lower	5	114	5	22.8	M
Wella Vidiya Roman Catholic Tamil	Lower	10	407	19	21.4	TC
Wella Vidiya Sinhala Mixed	Lower	10	1,075	30	35.8	S

S = Sinhala   M = Muslim   TC=Tamil Catholic

in staff-student ratio between the two types of schools.

The poor quality of education in Kamachchode can be best illustrated by examining in more detail the Kamachchode Muslim School. This school is situated on the northern border of the community. In 1984 the school was under an acting headmaster who happened to be a Sinhalese Catholic. Due to the scarcity of qualified Muslim teachers, a number of Sinhalese teachers had been posted to this school on a temporary basis. The school had suffered a number of setbacks in the past, including a gradual reduction in the number of grades available in the school right down to grade five. (About 10 years ago it had classes up to grade 10). While the school is now under government control, the only building in the school is said to be owned by the nearby mosque. This has resulted in a situation where neither the Education Department nor the mosque pays any attention to the required maintenance work on the building. The school does not have some of the basic facilities, including water supply, electricity or even latrines. The school is attended by Muslim children from Kamachchode and several other such communities. There is hardly any community support for any of the school activities. As a primary school, Kamachchode Muslim School is supposed to be preparing children for a higher grade Muslim school, i.e., the Alhilal Muslim College at Periyamulla, but as of 1984 only three children from Kamachchode were attending the latter school.

SUMMARY AND CONCLUSION

On the whole the literacy and the level of educational achievement among the watta-dwellers are quite low. In contrast, the level of primary school attendance among the watta children in compulsory school-going ages tends to be satisfactory. The low educational achievement of the watta-dwellers may be partly attributed to circumstances prevailing in watta communities, including poverty, use of child labor, the high rate of broken families and lack of parental and community support for education. However, certain imbalances in the educational delivery system in the urban areas appear to be equally if not more significant as regards the low educational achievement of the watta-dwellers.

This study identified a category of deprived schools in urban areas catering more or less exclusively to the urban poor. These deprived urban schools have the following characteristics.

1. The limitation of space and congestion, somewhat resembling the physical conditions prevailing in the watta communities.

2. Lack of basic amenities, educational equipment and sports and recreational facilities.

3. Heavy bias towards primary education and lack of integration with the mainstream educational institutions geared to higher education.

4. Lower enrollment of girls compared to boys [3].

5. Higher dropout rates especially in terminal grades in primary education.

6. The pattern of ethno-religious differentiation of the relevant schools.

The mechanisms through which these underprivileged schools exist side by side with the privileged ones within the same state-administered education system need to be carefully examined in future studies. In the short run there is an urgent need to upgrade facilities and quality of education in the so-called "watta schools". It may be possible to minimize the existing imbalances in the education system through the proposed "parsada system", whereby a linking of well-equipped and poorly-equipped schools in a given area is envisaged.

Finally, there are certain problems associated with the pattern of enthno-religious differentiation of schools at the watta level. Most importantly this tends to serve against ethnic harmony within the watta communities. In many ways the pattern of ethno-religious differentiation of schools is at odds with the ethnic intermixture, bilingualism and religious syncretism manifest in the watta communities as described in the previous chapters. Further, the existing system of primary education at the watta level may be uneconomical in so far as it gives rise to an uneconomical distribution of scarce educational resources among many small schools each catering to a small fragment of the local population. From all these angles, it will be desirable to evolve a system of primary education which facilitates an easy transfer to secondary education, promotes ethnic harmony and at the same time makes optimum use of the available educational resources for the benefit of the urban poor.

NOTES

1. It is possible that any educational high achievers from these communities gradually moved out of them. However, this study did not come across any actual instance where this has occurred.

2. As the medium of instruction in this school was Sinhala even Tamil and Muslim children in the school received their education in Sinhala.

3. This finding, while consistent with data on school dropouts in Jude Mawatha and Swarna Mawatha, is inconsistent with relevant data from Soyza Lane and Kamach-

chode. The lower dropout rate among girls relative to boys in Soyza Lane and Kamachchode may be due to special circumstances prevailing in these two communities. The demands of the informal sector in Soyza Lane and fishing industry in Kamachchode may be such that the boys in these two communities are compelled to drop out from school rather early.

CHAPTER SEVEN

ASPECTS OF COMMUNITY HEALTH

This chapter examines the health problems in the watta communities studied in relation to their economic, social, cultural and physical setting described in the earlier chapters. By now it is well known that both mortality and morbidity levels in watta communities are quite high relative to other types of rural and urban communities in Sri Lanka (Marga Institute 1982, Cassim et al. 1982, Tilakaratna et al. 1984). What factors contribute to the high levels of mortality and morbidity in these communities. This is the central issue addressed in the present chapter.

INFANT AND CHILD MORTALITY

When we look at the aggregate figures for all four communities, for every 10 children surviving up to five years of age, there is one infant or child death. Further, as much as 44 percent of all infant and child deaths in these communities occur during the first month of their life; 81 percent of them occur within the first year of their life. The highest incidence of infant and child mortality is in Jude Mawatha, followed by Soyza Lane, Swarna Mawatha and Kamachchode. In Jude Mawatha for every three children surviving up to age five, there is at least one infant or child death. On the whole the two inner-city slum communities have considerably higher infant and child mortality compared to the other two communities. As physical amenities in the latter two communities are in no way

179

better than those in the two slums, the higher infant and child mortality in the slums may be largely due to the higher degree of social disorganization, including the weaker family structure, characteristic of the slum.

In addition to infant and child deaths, abortions also appear to be rather common in watta communities. Even though the present study made no systematic effort to obtain data on prenatal deaths, miscarriages and abortions were frequently mentioned by mothers during informal conversations recorded in the field notebooks.

TABLE 7.1

INFANT AND CHILD DEATHS OVER A FIVE YEAR PERIOD
(1979 - 1984)

Age at Death	Number of Deaths				
	JM	SM	SL	KM	All
Less than 1 month	6	1	0	0	7
1 - 11 months	3	0	2	1	6
1 - 5 years	0	1	1	1	3
Total no. of deaths	9	2	3	2	16
Total no. of living	24	36	30	62	152
Ratio of living to one death	3	18	10	31	10

MORBIDITY PATTERN

Information on morbidity was obtained through the household survey. Each household was asked to indicate

TABLE 7.2

PREVALENCE OF SELECTED ILLNESSES*

Illness Category	JM f	JM %	SM f	SM %	SL f	SL %	KM f	KM %	All f	All %
Diarrhea	7	2.3	5	1.8	9	4.6	64	11.6	85	6.4
Common cold	18	6.0	32	11.6	30	15.4	103	18.6	183	13.8
Cough	6	2.0	24	8.7	1	0.5	8	1.4	39	2.9
TB	1	0.3	1	0.4	0	0	1	0.2	3	0.2
Asthma	0	0	7	2.5	2	1.0	1	0.2	10	0.7
Malaria	3	1.0	1	0.4	2	1.0	1	0.2	7	0.5
Fever	15	5.0	15	5.5	23	11.8	43	7.8	96	7.2
Scabies	4	1.3	5	1.8	4	2.0	4	0.7	17	1.3
Other skin disease	5	1.7	4	1.5	6	3.1	9	1.6	24	1.8
Measles	1	0.3	0	0	0	0	1	0.2	2	0.2
Eye infections	3	1.0	1	0.4	2	1.0	4	0.7	10	0.7
Worms	1	0.3	0	0	5	2.6	0	0	6	0.4
Home accidents	4	1.3	0	0	1	0.5	1	0.2	6	0.4
Fits	0	0	0	0	0	0	1	0.2	1	0.1
Other	8	2.6	7	2.5	4	2.0	12	2.2	31	2.3

* The percentages given here indicate the proportion of people in each community reporting a given illness over a one-month recall period.

the number of household members who received medica-
tion (including self-medication) for various illness
categories over a 30 day recall period. The resulting
data are presented in Table 7.2.

It must be noted that the procedure adopted here
clearly excluded a number of illness categories that
may be widely prevalent among the urban poor, among
them malnutrition, alcoholism, drug addiction and
sexually transmitted diseases. Seasonal changes in the
morbidity pattern too could not be established through
the above procedure. Leaving aside the above limitations, we can see that respiratory diseases (i.e.,
common cold, cough, TB and asthma) and diarrhea are
the commonest diseases in the communities studied.
While 17.6 percent of the total population covered in
this study reported respiratory infections of one kind
or another, diarrhea was reported by 6.4 percent of
the population for the one month reference period. The
highest prevalence of respiratory diseases is in
Swarna Mawatha, followed by Kamachchode, Soyza Lane
and Jude Mawatha. The prevalence of diarrhea is
highest in Kamachchode, followed by Soyza Lane, Jude
Mawatha and Swarna Mawatha.

Among the other illnesses reported, fever of
unknown origin is significant. There are a few cases
of infectious diseases including measles, scabies and
eye infections. The only reported vector-borne disease
is malaria but some of the fever cases especially in
Swarna Mawatha may be due to Dengue Hemorrhagic Fever.
Of the remaining illness categories, skin diseases and
worm infestations are more prevalent in Soyza Lane,
while home accidents are mostly found in Jude Mawatha.

We will now consider a broad range of factors
associated with the morbidity trends in the communities studied.

PREVENTIVE HEALTH SERVICES

The local municipal councils are responsible for the prevention of diseases and promotion of health in the watta communities. Each municipal council has a separate health department which is responsible among other things for maternal and child health, environmental sanitation, health education and prevention and control of epidemics in the watta communities. In the past the successful delivery of these services by the municipal councils had been hampered by the shortage of funds, shortage of staff and other administrative difficulties normally encountered by the municipal councils.

In 1973 the CAB was established to supplement municipal services to the urban poor; provision and maintenance of water taps, latrines and other publicly-used physical amenities serving the watta communities were made the specific responsibility of the CAB. Since 1979 an UNICEF-assisted Environmental Sanitation and Community Development Program involving both the CMC and CAB has been in operation in parts of the Colombo city (for details see Tilakaratna et al. 1984).

Of the four communities covered by this study, only Swarna Mawatha was served by the UNICEF-assisted special program. On the whole the public health activities serving the urban poor in Kandy and Negombo were restricted to the routine municipal services.

The frequency of contact between the public health staff and the study communities was assessed through the household survey. The relevant data are presented in Table 7.3.

183

TABLE 7.3

DISTRIBUTION OF HOUSEHOLDS ACCORDING TO FREQUENCY OF
CONTACT WITH PUBLIC HEALTH STAFF

Contact with public health staff	Jude Mawatha		Swarna Mawatha		Soyza Lane		Kamach- chode		Total	
	No.	%	No.	%	No.	%	No.	%	No.	%
Often	0	0	0	0	0	0	0	0	0	0
At times	12	24	16	31	24	73	63	76	115	53
Never	37	76	35	69	9	27	20	24	101	47
Total	49	100	51	100	33	100	83	100	216	100

It is evident that nearly 47 percent of all households surveyed have no contact whatsoever with the public health staff. The remaining 53 percent of the households have only occasional contact while none admitted to having frequent contact. The highest frequency of contact with the public health staff is in Kamachchode, followed by Soyza Lane, Swarna Mawatha and Jude Mawatha. Even though Swarna Mawatha is covered by the UNICEF-funded special program mentioned earlier, its reported contact with the public health staff remained rather limited as of 1983. On the whole the urban poor in the provincial towns like Kandy and Negombo tend to have better contact with public health staff compared to those in Colombo. Perhaps this may be due to a better staff-resident ratio in provincial towns as against Colombo. The mortality or morbidity trends in the study communities do not have any direct relationship to the level of contact with the public health staff.

CURATIVE HEALTH SERVICES

In this study no attempt was made to systematically follow up the nature of curative services utilized by the urban poor. However, some important features relating to the curative behavior of watta residents were observed in this study. One important finding is that 3.6 percent of the average monthly expenditure of a watta household is spent on medical expenses. It ranges from 1.7 percent in Swarna Mawatha to 4.8 percent in Jude Mawatha.

Free allopathic and Ayurvedic medical services are available within easy reach of each of the four communities studied. While the watta residents heavily utilize these free medical services, from time to time they also patronize private allopathic practitioners accessible to them. Apart from one or two abortionists and some occultists, there are no curative agents of any kind currently living in the communities studied. The home remedies used by the watta-dwellers too consist mostly of "shop medicines". These factors explain the relatively high medical expenses among the watta-dwellers.

ENVIRONMENTAL AND ECOLOGICAL FACTORS

Certain environmental and ecological factors which are typically associated with watta communities are critically important in the widespread prevalence of respiratory diseases in these communities. Limitation of living space, dampness, poor ventilation and other such conditions conducive to respiratory infections are found in varying degrees in all four communities studied. The communities with the highest prevalence of various respiratory infections, i.e., Swarna Mawatha and Kamachchode, also have a higher proportion of shanty type housing compared to the other communities; the proportion of shanty type housing in Swarna Mawatha, Kamachchode, Soyza Lane and Jude

Mawatha are 88 percent, 35 percent, 24 percent and 20 percent respectively.

Further, by virtue of their physical location Kamachchode and Swarna Mawatha are exposed to damp and marshy conditions associated with the sea and the canal respectively. During high tides sea water flows directly into certain shanties in Kamachchode. It is also significant that the lowest prevalence of respiratory diseases is found in Jude Mawatha, which is situated in a well-drained higher elevation. The findings of this study suggest that the respiratory diseases are more common in urban fringe communities as against inner-city slums, where conditions may be less favorable to this particular disease category.

DIETARY PATTERN

Certain special dietary practices prevalent in watta communities were identified in this study. One such practice is the widespread consumption of some cheap but filling food items like maniyok (cassava), sweet potatoes, maize and sago, both as a principal meal and as snacks. There is considerable variation in food habits among different watta communities, depending largely on the type of food that is locally available. For instance, in Kamachchode, where the primary economic activity is fishing, fish is highly important as a food item. The lower infant and child mortality in Kamachchode in turn may be partly due to the nutritional significance of fish in this community (see Table 7.1).

One important feature of the dietary practices in watta communities is their heavy reliance on cooked food sold by wayside boutiques and mobile vendors. Most households in Soyza Lane rarely cook meals at home as they are accustomed to obtaining cooked food from nearby hotels and eating houses. Some people in Soyza Lane, who work in these establishments, get a free supply of cooked food to be taken home or eaten within the premises. These practices illustrate links between the informal sector economy and food habits. Some other residents in Soyza Lane regularly patronize the local eateries for major meals, snacks and tea. Because of these practices some households in Soyza Lane have no facilities for cooking at all; lack of firewood, lack of cooking space, and other such environmental constraints typically associated with inner-city slums, combined with higher female participation in paid employment and their attitude towards domestic life, largely explain the lack of home cooking, including non-availability of boiled water in these communities. Some households in Soyza Lane have been without cooking for so long that the housewives there have completely lost their culinary skills.

In Kamachchode too, many households heavily rely on food vendors operating in the nearby fish market or on certain local households that sell home-cooked meals to others in the community, usually with prior arrangement. Any public health standards applicable to regular catering establishments are neither enforced nor heeded to in any of the above instances. The high diarrheal prevalence in Kamachchode and Soyza Lane, evident in Table 7.2, can be partly attributed to their heavy dependence on the informal sector supply of cooked meals.

PRACTICES RELATING TO DRINKING WATER

First we will examine the availability of safe drinking water in the communities studied.

It is clear from Table 7.4 that a vast majority of the households surveyed (i.e., 75 percent) obtain their drinking water from public water taps. Private water taps installed within houses are somewhat important in Jude Mawatha and Kamachchode. In addition

187

to this, there is one open well and several tube wells used by a total of six households in Kamachchode. The average number of households served by each public water tap ranges from 12 in Swarna Mawatha to 33 in Soyza Lane. In the former the water supply has substantially improved lately due to special UNICEF/CAB/CMC interventions.

TABLE 7.4

DISTRIBUTION OF HOUSEHOLDS ACCORDING TO
SOURCE OF DRINKING WATER

Source of Drinking Water	JM		SM		SL		KM		Total	
	f	%	f	%	f	%	f	%	f	%
Private Tap	19	39	2	4	0	0	27	33	48	22.2
Public Tap	30	61	49	96	33	100	50	60	162	75.0
Well	0	0	0	0	0	0	1	1	1	0.5
Other	0	0	0	0	0	0	5	6	5	2.3
Total	49	100	51	100	33	100	83	100	216	100.0

To what extent is the advice given by public health authorities concerning the preparation of drinking water practiced by the watta-dwellers? The relevant data are presented in Table 7.5.

Only 11 percent of all households surveyed stated that they always consumed boiled-cooled water. While another 11 percent stated that they often take boiled-cooled water, some 66 percent of the households reported that they take boiled-cooled water only

188

occasionally. During informal discussions many people expressed the view that consumption of boiled water is only required at times of illness. This tallies with the high proportion of households reporting only occasional use of boiled-cooled water. The responses of the watta residents are consistent with a widespread cultural belief in Sri Lanka which holds that taking of boiled water is a remedy for certain types of illness rather than a general precaution against water-borne diseases (for details see Nickter 1987). Finally, the practical difficulties in preparing boiled water in the watta context, as also manifested in a lack of home cooking in some of the communities, should not be overlooked.

TABLE 7.5

DISTRIBUTION OF HOUSEHOLDS ACCORDING TO THE
FREQUENCY OF DRINKING BOILED-COOLED WATER

Frequency of drinking boiled cooled water	Jude Mawatha		Swarna Mawatha		Soyza Lane		Kamach-chode		Total	
	f	%	f	%	f	%	f	%	f	%
Always	2	4	17	33	2	6	3	4	24	11
Often	2	4	5	10	6	18	11	13	24	11
Seldom	43	88	23	45	13	40	63	76	142	66
Never	2	4	6	12	12	36	6	7	26	12
Total	49	100	51	100	33	100	83	100	216	100

Of the communities studied, the highest frequency of drinking boiled-cooled water is reported in Swarna Mawatha. This in turn may be seen as an outcome of the UNICEF/CAB/CMC interventions in this community. It shows that the practice of drinking boiled water can be popularized in these communities provided that they are made to understand its preventive value.

TOILET PRACTICES

Data on toilet practices in the study communities are presented in Tables 7.6 and 7.7.

TABLE   7.6

DISTRIBUTION OF HOUSEHOLDS ACCORDING
TO THE PLACE OF DEFECATION

Place of Defecation	Jude Mawatha		Swarna Mawatha		Soyza Lane		Kamach-chode		Total	
	f	%	f	%	f	%	f	%	f	%
Private latrine	15	31	0	0	0	0	26	31	41	19
Public latrine	34	69	49	96	33	100	33	40	149	69
Beach, canal etc.	0	0	2	4	0	0	24	29	26	12
Total	49	100	51	100	33	100	83	100	216	100

Table 7.6 shows that in the study communities, public latrines are most widely used, followed by private household latrines and open spaces. With regard to the type of latrines used a vast majority of households in all communities studied reported using water seal latrines. Common latrines in all four communities studied are of the water seal type. Their quality and nature of use, however, vary considerably. There is considerable variation in toilet practices

190

between Kamachchode and Swarna Mawatha, the communities reporting the highest and the lowest prevalence of diarrhea respectively (see Table 7.2). In comparing the toilet practices in Kamachchode and Swarna Mawatha, we must remember that the two communities have several features in common including the significance of shanty-type housing in each community.

TABLE 7.7

DISTRIBUTION OF HOUSEHOLDS ACCORDING
TO TYPE OF LATRINE USED

Type of latrine	Jude Mawatha f	Jude Mawatha %	Swarna Mawatha f	Swarna Mawatha %	Soyza Lane f	Soyza Lane %	Kamach- chode f	Kamach- chode %	Total f	Total %
Water seal	46	94	49	96	33	100	51	62	179	83
Bucket	1	2	0	0	0	0	0	0	1	0
Cesspit	2	4	0	0	0	0	6	7	8	4
Other	0	0	2	4	0	0	26	31	28	13
Total	49	100	51	100	33	100	83	100	216	100

In Swarna Mawatha both toilet facilities and their utilization have considerably improved since 1980 due to UNICEF/CAB/CMC special interventions mentioned earlier. Before 1980 the people of Swarna Mawatha defecated along the canal either in the open or in tiny shelters with ditches draining to the canal. Following the construction of public latrines (water seal type) in 1980 the community has gradually adopted the practice of using public latrines. Some persuasion by community leaders and the rapid construction of houses along the canal bank restricting the number of secluded places used for defecation were important factors in the community's rapid transition towards using public latrines. The lower prevalence of

191

diarrhea in Swarna Mawatha in turn can be seen as an outcome of the above changes in toilet practices.

In contrast, a good number of people in Kamachchode continue to use the beach as their regular place of defecation. Worse still the same beach is used for unloading, packing and the market display of fresh fish as well as in the processing of dried fish. The high prevalence of diarrhea in Kamachchode may or may not be associated with the above practices. The seemingly unhygienic toilet practices in Kamachchode cannot be attributed solely to the nature of toilet facilities locally available. As in Swarna Mawatha in Kamachchode, too, the toilet facilities have improved. The houses in the Municipal Housing Project have been provided with separate latrine units. Moreover, certain public latrines have been built by the Municipality for the benefit of shanty dwellers. Both the quality and quantity of latrines in Kamachchode are superior to those in Jude Mawatha or Soyza Lane and comparable to those in Swarna Mawatha.

Therefore, the differences in toilet practices between Kamachchode and Swarna Mawatha cannot be attributed to any marked difference in the type and quality of toilet facilities available in the two communities. It shows that custom and habit, as well as the nature of toilet facilities available, affect the toilet practices in watta communities.

SUMMARY AND CONCLUSION

The health profile of watta communities studied is marked by high infant mortality and widespread prevalence of respiratory infections and diarrheal diseases. These features in turn may be attributed to a variety of factors, including the quality of health services catering to the particular target group, poor housing and environmental conditions, lack of safe drinking water and inadequate toilet facilities,

culturally or practically determined dietary practices, toilet habits and attitudes towards drinking
water and the nature of social organization, family
life and economic activities in the relevant communities. Further, our analysis of the household
expenditure pattern in Chapter Three suggests that
alcoholism, smoking, drug addiction and betel chewing
are considerably common in the watta communities. All
these point to the need for employing an intersectoral
approach in dealing with health problems among the
urban poor in Sri Lanka.

CHAPTER EIGHT

CONCLUSION

Many studies on the urban poor in the Third World stress their recent rural origin and continuing ties with the rural areas. This is evident from labels, such as "Peasants in Cities" (Mangin 1970), "Cities of Peasants" (Roberts 1978) and "Rural Transplants" (Breese 1966). Their organization into urban communities is mainly seen as an outcome of both their common rural origin and the common problems experienced by them in making their transition to the city (Little 1964, Breese 1966). Anthropologists, in particular, have highlighted the manner in which this transition is facilitated by kinship, caste, ethnicity and other social arrangements rooted in the rural origins of these city dwellers (Rowe 1973, Shack 1973).

The watta communities of Sri lanka, described in the preceding chapters, do not confirm to this model in some important respects. Direct migration from rural areas have only marginally contributed to the growth of watta communities in recent years. Only about 16 percent of all household heads in the four communities studied reported that they were born in villages or plantations; the rest had originated in urban centers of some sort. Moreover, the wattas had relatively few ongoing links with rural areas in the forms of migrations, social visits, exchanges etc. The only exception was the Swarna Mawatha community which had received a stream of migration from the plantation areas following the land reforms of 1975, which had a destabilizing effect on a section of the plantation workers who were of Indian origin.

As we saw in Chapter One, there has been a slow to moderate growth of major urban centers in Sri Lanka since its political independence from Britain in 1948. The rural-oriented development policies pursued by successive governments in independent Sri Lanka resulted in a limited flow of rural-urban migration as compared to other countries in the Third World. The liberalized economic policies implemented in Sri Lanka since 1977 have not transformed the existing pattern of urbanization.

A slow rate of urbanization, however, has been accompanied by a disproportionate growth in the number of urban poor, particularly in Colombo. It appears that besides rural-urban migration, natural growth and increased class differentiation within cities have been equally, if not more significant, in the evolution of the watta communities. For example, the surplus population in inner-city slums, which had evolved throughout the colonial era, contributed much to the formation of the shanty wattas during the post-independence period. Mainly due to the absence of a massive influx of rural migrants, the individual watta communities remain relatively small, the average number of people in a community studied being 332 [1].

It follows that the community organization of the watta-dwellers cannot be treated as an aspect of their rural heritage; rather, it is something that evolves through their shared experiences in dealing with the common problems encountered by them within the urban society itself. Both, through their origin and present circumstances, many of them are intensely urban and, one might even say, directly linked to the global processes since they have merged with an international mobility of labor directed to the

196

Middle East. Hence we may now focus on large scale urban processes influencing the formation and persistence of the watta communities.

In trying to understand the wider urban context of the wattas, to some extent, we can utilize the theory of urban system developed by Castells (1977, 1978, 1983). As outlined in Chapter One, Castells saw the urban system in modern capitalist societies as a means of ensuring reproduction of labor power for the benefit of capitalism. Therefore, according to Castells, the provision of basic urban services, such as facilities for housing construction, and health, educational and recreational facilities, is a key function of the urban system. He also perceived that there are inherent contradictions within a capitalist urban system since a diversion of capital is needed for ensuring reproduction of labor power. By controlling the provision and "social consumption" of essential urban services, the state directly intervenes in the process of reproduction of labor power in order to ensure that capitalist requirements for a disciplined and productive work force are met. This situation produces inherent contradictions between the state and the city-dwellers, contradictions that are parallel to, but not identical with those of class conflict. The resulting protest manifests itself mainly through what Castells terms "urban social movements".

According to Castells, urban social movements are "urban-oriented mobilizations that influence structural social change and transform the urban meanings" (1983: 303). Examples of such movements are squatters' movements, campaigns against slum clearance, feminist movements, and a variety of citizens' associations typically found in modern cities.

197

While Castells formulated his theory of urban system mainly by reference to developed western societies, he also applied it in a limited way to Latin America. In his view, while shantytowns in Third World cities manifest sharp social contradictions, they exist at the bottom end of a chain of dependencies that restrict their ability to resist and transform the system via urban social movements. To him, a Third World city is a "dependent city" in that it is structurally subordinate to centers of growth elsewhere.

> The dependent city is the ecological form resulting from the resident's lack of social control over urban development because of their forced submission to the good will of the state and to the changing flows of foreign capital. The dependent city is a city without citizens (Castells 1983: 212).

Neither Castells nor his critics (e.g. Lowe 1986) seriously addressed the complexities involved in the application of his theory to the so-called "dependent city". One problematic area is the nature of the state in Third World societies and its relation to the process of reproduction of labor power within the relevant urban contexts. Also, the specific role of residential communities particularly within the Third World cities remains unclarified. In his earlier writings Castells dismissed studies of urban communities, saying that they were a legacy of the Chicago School (Castells 1977, 1978). However, he rediscovered urban communities in his later research as he found that "community building" is the aim and indeed, a positive outcome of a certain type of urban social movement (Castells 1983).

The two types of urban low-income communities found in Sri Lanka — the slum wattas and shanty wattas — may be seen as a social arrangement for reproduction of labor power involving a minimum cost to the state. The watta-dwellers occupy low-cost houses, built mostly by themselves on marginal urban land for which there are no alternative uses. The organization of watta households, kinship networks and forms of reciprocity in turn facilitate the reconstitution of an urban work force with minimum inputs from the state. Some of the key services required for reconstitution of this work force are provided cheaply by the branches of the informal sector built around the watta communities. This includes the provision of cooked food, particularly for those having no tradition of home cooking.

In this context, the intervention by the state in the reproduction of an urban work force is often of an indirect nature. With their gradual incorporation by the state, the wattas receive a minimum of essential urban services, such as common latrines, common taps and rudimentary educational and recreational facilities. It is important that these services are provided on a communal basis in ways that reinforce the structure of the community. Indeed the formation of a Community Development Council (CDC) has been stipulated as a pre-condition for installation of basic common amenities in the wattas in the recent effort to upgrade the services provided to them by the state (Thilakaratna et al. 1984). Also, as we have seen, the ethnic divisions within the wattas are reinforced by the state educational system, which provides the watta-dwellers essentially a watta-specific ethnic education.

What emerges from the present study is that, particularly among the poorer inhabitants in Third World cities, the reproduction of labor power and reproduction of the community are closely interconnected. These two processes appear to be mediated and facilitated by the state in varying degrees. The communities have evolved and are being maintained as a cheap source of labor that may be exploited by local and international capital when needed. Therefore, the persistence of these communities is not so much through a perpetual culture of poverty embedded in them, as through certain macro processes mediated by the state. In this sense, such communities are a product of state policy as much as they are an outcome of certain "natural" social processes (Suttles 1972).

It may be argued that from the angle of national and international capital, the watta work force is superfluous since the watta-dwellers are by and large informal sector workers. This is indeed the position of many authorities on such communities in Latin America (e.g. Quijano 1974, Eckstein 1975). However, the considerable flow of female labor from the wattas to the Middle East indicates that the wattas are firmly within the orbit of international capital. Some of the foreign-owned manufacturing and processing plants in the Free Trade Zone opened up in Sri Lanka since 1978 have also absorbed some workers from the wattas [2]. Hence the watta-dwellers constitute more than a "reserve army of labor" in relation to international capital. A small, but perhaps an increasing number of them are directly employed by local and international capital.

There are also certain indirect benefits derived by the formal sector through the informal sector as noted by Roberts (1978) for Latin America [3]. For instance, services rendered by housemaids from the wattas enable middle-class women to work in the formal sector on a full-time basis. Similarly, informal sector services, such as laundry work, repairing of shoes, food vending and transport of goods and people often benefit the formal sector workers. While it may be that generally the less profitable and socially unattractive economic activities are the ones left to the informal sector, we found a considerable dynamism within it. The pattern of social mobility exemplified by Akman, a fruit vendor from Soyza Lane, Kandy, the determination of the watta youths to excel in the football game, the rush for Middle-East employment among the watta women and the kind of social processes the watta-dwellers like to view on the movie screen, all indicate a strong desire for upward social mobility in spite of limited opportunities. This element of dynamism and social mobility, also noted by several other observers on Third World cities (e.g. Turner 1967, 1977; Mangin 1973; Santos 1979), has received insufficient attention in both culture of poverty and dependency theories.

Finally, what conclusions may be drawn from the present study regarding the nature of the urban protest in the Third World? Apart from general manifestations of social stress, such as crime, alcoholism, gang activities and the like, this study came across three instances of protest within the communities studied. First, the persistent but ultimately unsuccessful struggle by the dwellers of Soyza Lane to protect their community and the right to survive within the city center.

The whole community participated in this struggle, but it was an isolated campaign, unrelated to any broader political processes involving a mass of city dwellers. In this campaign the community leaders firmly and vigorously expressed their grievances to local and national politicians with whom they had contacts of some sort. Theirs was chiefly a struggle for retaining their homes; it also sought to retain their control over certain business locations in the city that were strategically important in pavement hawking. However, in the end capital prevailed over the wishes of these slum-dwellers who

201

were forcibly moved out of their central-city location which had been newly earmarked for a super-
market. There was no effort on the part of the
people of Soyza Lane to transform the urban structure or urban meaning; they merely sought to retain
their position within the existing urban structure.
Hence, theirs was an urban protest not leading to an
urban social movement as defined by Castells.

As another instance of an urban struggle, the
UPON in Negombo was considerably more organized than
the Soyza Lane campaign. It sought to unite all
watta-dwellers in Negombo in a collective effort to
improve their living conditions. It addressed a
whole range of watta problems, including housing,
unemployment, indebtedness, alcoholism, marital
instability and juvenile delinquency. To the extent
it was a church-sponsored self-help movement, it did
not challenge the existing urban structure.

However, it had acquired some degree of mili-
tancy through its struggles against the municipality
and local business interests represented by tourist
hoteliers in its efforts to secure land and capital
for housing projects for the urban poor. Here too,
as in Soyza Lane, the demands arising from the
process of reproduction of labor power within the
wattas came in conflict with the interests of the
dominant classes. To the extent UPON would be able
to transform the power structure of the city to the
advantage of the watta-dwellers, it had the potential of becoming an urban social movement. However,
such an eventuality was by no means certain, given
the organizational and ideological problems it was
facing.

Since the watta-dwellers played a prominent role
in the nationwide riots of July 1983, it may also be
seen as a manifestation of urban protest. As far as
the wattas were concerned, it was a more or less

spontaneous outbreak of looting and street violence primarily directed against a section of the urban elite. Even though their ethnic sentiments had been aroused, their chief aims were rampaging and looting, their hostilities being primarily directed against a section of the affluent who were defenseless at the time. The riots gave expression to a situation where class cleavages and what Castells terms "consumption cleavages" became temporarily merged with ethnic cleavages at least in the minds of the watta-dwellers who took part in these riots [4].

At the inception the state tended to turn a blind eye towards the rioters, but as the riots spread widely posing a threat to the entire social order, the state vigorously and hurriedly repressed rioting. In the end these riots only resulted in an increased police vigilance over the wattas. In contrast to urban social movements, these riots were merely destructive and in no way ushered in a new social order. It also showed the incongruous nature of the relationship between the state and the wattas; the state, while tolerating or even sustaining the wattas (as they are) when they do not pose a threat to the city establishment, quickly resorts to repression when the wattas become active in urban protest.

Thus while urban protest occurs frequently in Third World cities, it may lead to urban social movements only under exceptionally favorable circumstances. The Third World city may be a city without citizens as noted by Castells. However, it is a city made up of vibrant communities engaged in dynamic interaction with one another and with the state. What happens to, and in such communities is as important as the dynamics of world capitalism in determining the future of Third World cities.

NOTES

1. There is, however, a few exceptionally large watta communities in each of the major cities, for example, Wanathamulla in Colombo and Mahaiyawa in Kandy. None of these exceptionally large watta communities was included in the present study.

2. The study came across a total of 11 Free Trade Zone workers in Jude Mawatha and Kamachchode situated some 10 to 20 kilometers away from the Free Trade Zone. There was none working in the Free Trade Zone in the other two study communities which were situated over 30 kilometers away from the Free Trade Zone.

3. See also the findings of Forbes (1981) regarding petty commodity production in Indonesia.

4. For similar observations on urban riots in the US during the 1960s see Banfield 1968 and Wilson 1970.

BIBLIOGRAPHY

Abeysekera, D.
1980 Urbanization and Growth of Small Towns in Sri Lanka, 1901-71. Honolulu: East-West Center. (Papers of the East West Population Institute, No. 67).

Adams, R.
1974 Harnessing Technical Development. in J.J. Poggie & R.N. Lynch eds. Rethinking Modernization: Anthropological Perspectives. Westport, CT: Greenwood Press. pp. 83-99.

Adamson, P.
1982 The Gardens. New Internationalist 109: 7-28.

Ariyaratne, M.H.E.
1979 Study of a Metropolitan Location with Residential Predominance by an Ethnic Minority. in Marga Institute,, 1979 b, pp. 198-220.

Bandusena, M.
1983 The Informal Sector in Urban Areas: A Physical Planning Approach. Katubedda: University of Moratuwa, Dissertation for Diploma in Urban Development.

205

Banfield, E.C.
1968   The Unheavenly City: The Nature and
               Future of Our Urban Crisis. Boston:
               Little, Brown and Company.

Breese, G.
1966   Urbanization   in   Newly   Developing
               Countries. Englewood   Cliffs,   NJ:
               Prentice Hall.

Brett, S.
1974   Low Income Urban Settlements in Latin
               America: The Turner Model. in E. de
               Kadt & G. Williams eds. Sociology and
               Development. London: Tavistock. pp.
               171-96.

Bulankulame,
P.S.W. et al.
1978   City of Colombo, Sri Lanka: The
               Integration of Squatters into the
               Mainstream of Urban Life. in The Role
               of Housing in Promoting Social Integra-
               tion. New York: UN. pp. 165-97.

Casinader, R.
& Ellepola, M.D.
1979   Migration and the Informal Sector. in
               Marga Institute 1979b. pp. 234-42.

Cassim, J.K.
et al.
1982   Development Councils for Participato-
               ry Urban Planning, Colombo, Sri Lanka.
               Assignment Children 57/58: 157-87.

Castells, M.
1977   The Urban Question: A Marxist Approach.
               London: Edward Arnold.

1978   City, Class and Power. London: Macmil-
                lan.

1983   The City and the Grassroots. London:
                Edward Arnold.

Chandrasiri, W.
    1982   A Community Development Program for
                 Shanty Settlements in the City of
                 Colombo. Katubedda: University of
                 Moratuwa, Dissertation for Diploma in
                 Urban Development.

Colombo Master
Plan Project
    1977   Policy Proposal Memorandum on Low-
                 income Housing and Shanty Resettlement
                 Program. Colombo: Dept. of Town and
                 Country Planning.

    1978   Colombo Metropolitan Region Urban
                 Development Plan. Colombo: Min. of
                 Local Government., Housing & Construc-
                 tion.

De Tissera, C.H.
& Ganesan, S.
    1978   Urban Housing for Low Income Groups.
                 Economic Review 3(11): 21-24.

Dias, E.
    1976   A Study of Slums and Shanties in the
                 City of Colombo. in Population Problem
                 in Sri Lanka. Colombo: Demographic
                 Research and Training Institute,
                 University of Colombo. pp. 66-67.

Eckstein, S.
1975   The Political Economy of Lower Class
        Areas in Mexico City: Societal
        Constraints on Local Business Oppor-
        tunities. Latin American Urban Research
        5: 125-45.

Fernando, M.W.
1979   Report of a Baseline Survey of the
        Shanty at Kirillapone. Colombo: Marga
        Institute.

Forbes, D.
1981   Petty Commodity Production and Under-
        development: The Case of Peddlers and
        Trishaw Riders in Ujung Pandang, In-
        donesia. Progress in Planning 16(2):
        107-167.

Gunatilake, G.
1973   The Rural-Urban Balance and Develop-
        ment: The Experience in Sri Lanka.
        Marga 2(1): 35-68.

Hechter, M.
1978   Group Formation and Cultural Division
        of Labor. American Journal of Sociology
        84(2): 293-318.

Jayasooriya, J.E.
1955   Children of the Slums. Journal of
        National Educational Society in Ceylon
        4(3): 21-28.

Jayasooriya, J.E.
& Kariyawasam, T.
1958   Juvenile Delinquency as a Gang Activity
        in the City of Colombo. Ceylon Journal
        of Historical and Social Studies 1(2):
        203-15.

Jayawardena, K.
1972   The Rise of the Labor Movement in
            Ceylon. Durham, N.C.: Duke University
            Press.

Kandiah, S.
1975   Review of Available Literature on
            Shanties in the City of Colombo.
            Katubedda: University of Moratuwa, MSc
            Thesis.

Kapferer, B.
1977   Marginality? Processes of Urban In-
            tegration and the Urban Poor. A Paper
            read at the Burg Wartenstein Symposium.
            No. 73, 1-10 July, 1977.

1983   A Celebration of Demons. Bloomington:
            Indiana University Press.

1988   Legends of People - Myths of State:
            Violence, Intolerance and Political
            Culture in Sri Lanka and Australia.
            Washington: Smithsonian Institution
            Press.

Karunaratne, W.
1983   Urban Development in the Slums and
            Shanties of Colombo, Sri Lanka.
            Development: Seeds of Change 2: 65-67.

Karunatilake,
H.N.S.
1981   Urbanization in Sri Lanka. Sri Lanka
            Journal of Social Science 4 (2): 35-
            46.

Karunatilleke,
A.V.G.C.
1978   Development Plan for Selected Shanty
            Communities of Colombo City. University
            of Moratuwa, MSc Thesis.

1979   The Shanty Communities of Colombo City
            with Special Reference to Two Loca-
            tions. in Marga Institute. 1979b. pp
            140-61.

Kurukulasuriya,
G.I.O.M.
1979   Poverty and the Urban-Rural Relation-
            ship in Sri Lanka. in Marga Institute,
            1979b. pp. 87-133.

Lankatilake,
A.L.B.
1976   A Housing Strategy for the Urban Poor.
            Katubedda: University of Moratuwa, MSc
            Thesis.

Lewis, O.
1959   Five Families: Mexican Case Studies in
            the Culture of Poverty. New York: Basic
            Books.

1965   La   Vida.   London: Panther   Modern
            Society.

Little, K.
1964   The Role of Voluntary Associations in
            West African Urbanization. in S.N.
            Eisenstadt ed. Contemporary Social
            Problems. New York: Free Press. pp.
            369-80.

Lomnitz, L.A.
1977   Networks and Marginality: Life in a
            Mexican Shantytown. New York: Academic
            Press.

Lowe, S.
1986   Urban Social Movements: The City After
            Castells. London: Macmillan.

Manatunga, P.W.
1982   The Extent of Participation in Formal
            Education by Dwellers of Shanties in a
            Slum Area of Colombo City. Colombo:
            University of Colombo, MSc Thesis.

Mangin, W. (ed.)
1970   Peasants in Cities: Readings in the
            Anthropology of Urbanization. Boston:
            Houghton Mifflin.

1973   Squatter Settlements. in Cities: Their
            Origin, Growth and Human Impact. San
            Francisco: W.H.Freeman. pp. 233-40.

Marga Institute
1976   Housing in Sri Lanka. Colombo: Marga
            Institute.

1979a   The Informal Sector of Colombo City.
            Colombo: Marga Institute.

1979b   UNCRD Research Project (Final Report)
            on Rural-Urban Relations: The Sri Lanka
            Case Study. Colombo: Marga Institute.

1982   Inter-City Workshop on PHC in Urban
            Areas: Colombo City Information Docu-
            ment. Colombo: Marga Institute.

McGee, T.G.
1971   Catalysts or Cancers? The Role of
             Cities in Asian Society. in L. Jakob-
             son & V. Prakash eds. Urbanization and
             National Development. Beverly Hills:
             Sage. pp. 157-81.

Mendis, W.M.J.G.
1976   A Case Study of the Colombo Community
             Development Society: An Innovative
             Example of a Strategy to Eradicate
             Urban Poverty in Sri Lanka. Katubedda,
             University of Moratuwa (mimeo).

1977   Social Organization of Squatter Settle-
             ments in the City of Colombo. A Paper
             read at the "Regional Seminar on Access
             to Basic Needs in Asian Squatter
             Settlements" organized by the Asian
             Council for Law and Development.

Mendis, M.W.J.G. &
Ranbanda, A.A.M.
1983   A Bibliography of the Research Publica-
             tions of the Department of Town and
             Country Planning, University of
             Moratuwa. Katubedda: University of
             Moratuwa.

Mendis, M.W.J.G.
& Rubasingham, S.
1982   A Select Bibliography of Recent Publi-
             cations on Urbanization and Urban
             Development in Sri Lanka. Katubedda:
             University of Moratuwa (mimeo).

Ministry of
Housing
1983   Urban Shelter Policy: Part 1 - Low
             Income Housing (mimeo).

Nelson, J.M.
1969 Migrants, Urban Poverty and Instability in Developing Nations. Cambridge: Harvard University Press.

Nickter, M.
1987 Cultural Dimensions of Hot, Cold and Sema in Sinhalese Health Culture. Social Science and Medicine 25(4): 377-87.

Nissan, E. &
Stirrat, R.L.
1987 State, Nation and the Representation of Evil: The Case Study of Sri Lanka. Brighton: University of Sussex. (Sussex Research Papers in Social Anthropology No.1).

Payne, G.K.
1977 Urban Housing in the Third World. London: Leonard Hill.

Perera, A.C.S.
1979 A Critique of the Informal Sector Concept in Relation to Employment in the City of Colombo, Sri Lanka. University College, London (unpublished).

1981 Conceptual Validity of the Informal Sector, Colombo City. A Paper read at SLAAS Annual Sessions, 1981.

1981 The Informal Sector : A Critique. Development Planning Review 1(1 & 2): 26-40.

Perera, N.B.
1973   Report of the Survey of Shanties in the
              City of Colombo. Colombo: CMC.

Perlman, J.E.
1976   The Myth of Marginality: Urban Poverty
              and Politics in Rio de Janeiro. Berke-
              ley; University of California Press.

Quijano, A.
1974   The Marginal Pole of the Economy and
              the Marginalized Labor Force. Economy
              and Society 3(4): 398-428.

Radampola, J. &
Selvarajah, E.
1977   A Community Development Program for
              Innercity Areas. A Case Study of
              Jintupitiya in the City of Colombo.
              Katubedda: University of Moratuwa, MSc
              Thesis.

Roberts, B
1978   Cities of Peasants: The Political
              Economy of Urbanization in the Third
              World. London: Edward Arnold.

Rodell, M.J.
1980   Colombo, Sri Lanka. in Policies Towards
              Urban Slums. Bangkok: ESCAP. pp. 22-
              41.

Rowe, W.L.
1973   Caste, Kinship and Association in Urban
              India. in A. Southhall ed. Urban
              Anthropology. New York: Oxford Univer-
              sity Press. pp 211-50.

Santos, M.
1979   The Shared Space: The Two Circuits of
            the Urban Economy in Underdeveloped
            Countries. London: Nethuen.

Selvarajah, E.
1983   The Impact of the Ceiling on Housing
            Property Law on the Slum and Shanty
            Program in Sri Lanka in S. Angel et al.
            eds. Land for Housing the Poor.
            Singapore: Select Books. pp 156-78.

Shack, W.A.
1973   Urban Ethnicity and the Cultural
            Process of Urbanization in Ethiopia in
            A. Southall ed. Urban Anthropology. New
            York: Oxford University Press. pp 251-
            256.

Silva, K.T.
1984   Report of the Sri Lanka Needs Assess-
            ment Survey. Kandy: Plan International.

1985   Prostitution in Sri Lanka. A Paper read
            at the Workshop of Experts on Preven-
            tion and Rehabilitation Schemes for
            Young Women in Prostitution and Related
            Occupations. Bangkok: ESCAP, 17 to 21
            June, 1985.

1986   Culture, Ecology and the Disease
            Pattern among the Urban Poor in Sri
            Lanka. Proceedings of the Second Asian
            Conference on Health and Medical
            Sociology, Urayasu City, Japan, 11-14
            August, 1986, pp. 71-76.

Siriwardena, S.
1985   Reflections on the Implementation of
            the Million Houses Program, Sri Lanka.
            Paper read at the International Sym-
            posium for Implementation of a Support
            Policy for Housing, November 1985.

Steinberg, F.
1982   Slum and Shanty Upgrading in Colombo.
            A Help for Urban Poor? International
            Journal of Urban & Regional Research
            6(3): 372-92.

1983   Better Housing for Colombo's Urban
            Poor. Open House 7(3): 37-49.

Suttles, G.D.
1972   The Social Construction of Communities.
            Chicago: University of Chicago Press.

Tambiah, S.J.
1957   A Sociological Approach to the Problem
            of Crime: A Study of Criminal Behavior
            Resulting from Social Disruptions and
            Deviational Pressures under Slum Condi-
            tions. Probation and Child Care 1(2):
            20-27.

1986   Sri Lanka: Ethnic Fratricide and the
            Dismantling of Democracy. Chicago:
            University of Chicago Press.

Tilakaratna, S.
et al.
1984   UNICEF Assisted Project on the Environ-
            mental Health and Community Development
            in the Slums and Shanties of the
            Colombo City (1979-83): An Evaluation
            Study. Colombo: UNICEF.

Turner, J.F.C.
1987   Barriers and Channels for Housing Development in Modernizing Countries. <u>Journal of the American Institute of Planners</u> 32(3): 167-81.

1970a   Squatter Settlements in Developing Countries. <u>in</u> D.P. Moynihan ed. Towards A National Urban Policy. New York: Basic Books. pp. 71-89.

1970b   Alternative Interpretations and Alternative Policies for Low-Income Housing in Transitional Economies. USAID Workshop on Squatter Settlements. Washington D.C. 3-7 Nov., 1970.

1977   Housing by People: Towards Autonomy in Building Environments. New York: Pantheon.

Urban Development
Authority
1979   Policy Paper on Slum and Shanty Upgrading in Colombo Municipal Council. Colombo: UDA (mimeo).

1982   Slum and Shanty Division of the Urban Development Authority: Program Summary up to November 1982. Colombo: UDA.

UNICEF
1983   Survey Study of the Colombo Urban Project. Colombo: UNICEF (mimeo).

1987   Plan of Action: Urban Basic Services Program (1979 to 1983). Colombo: UNICEF, 28 May, 1987.

Vidanagamachchi, S.
  1981   A Critical Appraisal of the Informal
              Sector in the City of Colombo. Katu-
              bedda: University of Moratuwa, MSc
              Thesis.

Wantawin, S.
  1982   Employment and Informal Sector Acti-
              vities of Slum and Shanty Residents: A
              Case Study of Two Shanty Settlements
              in Colombo, Sri Lanka. Bangkok: Asian
              Institute of Technology, Post-graduate
              Dissertation.

Wilson, J.Q.
  1970   Why We are Having a Wave of Violence.
              in N. Glazer ed. Cities in Trouble.
              Chicago: Quadrangle Books. pp. 55-56.

INDEX

219

About the Authors

Kalinga Tudor Silva holds a BA from University of Peradeniya, Sri Lanka, and PhD from Monash University, Australia. Presently he serves as Senior Lecturer and Head, Department of Sociology, University of Peradeniya. The senior author of <u>Malaria Control through Community Action at the Grass-roots</u> published in 1988 by the WHO and a co-editor of <u>Modern Sri Lanka Studies</u> published biannually by University of Peradeniya, Dr. Silva has published widely in Sri Lanka and abroad on a variety of subjects, including Social Change, Class Relations, Caste, Sociology of Health and Social Problems.

Karunatissa Athukorala, a BA honors graduate from University of Peradeniya, is a Lecturer in Sociology at the same university. An authority on youth problems in Sri Lanka, he has served as a Sociologist in the FINNIDA-funded Kandy District Water Supply and Sanitation Project and a consultant to the Ministry of Youth Affairs, Sri Lanka. In his latest research he explores the social history of gem miners in Sri Lanka.